Your Heart's Desire

YOUR HEART'S DESIRE

14 TRUTHS

*that will forever change
the way you love
and are loved*

·····························

Sheri Rose
SHEPHERD

·····························

TYNDALE™
MOMENTUM

An imprint of Tyndale House Publishers, Inc.

Library of Congress Cataloging-in-Publication Data

Shepherd, Sheri Rose, date.
  Your heart's desire : 14 truths that will forever change the way you love and are loved / Sheri Rose Shepherd.
    p. cm.
  Includes bibliographical references (p.   ).
  ISBN 978-1-4143-6691-3 (sc)
  1. Christian women—Religious life. 2. God (Christianity)—Love. 3. Love—Religious aspects—Christianity. I. Title.
  BV4529.S4315 2012
  248.8'43—dc23   2012004755

Printed in the United States of America

18	17	16	15	14	13	12
7	6	5	4	3	2	1

CONTENTS

FROM THE HEART OF
Sheri Rose

*Delight yourself in the LORD, and he will give
you the desires of your heart.*

PSALM 37:4, ESV

IF YOU HAVE PICKED up this book, it is probably for you. . . .

It is written for every woman who has ever loved a man. It is written for the married woman who loves her man but struggles in her marriage. It is written for the single woman who desires to find a good man to love her. It is written for the divorced woman who believed in her marriage only to have her man walk out. It is written for the mothers of sons who desire their beloved boys to become men of faith. This book is written for you and every woman who wants to find the courage to take a step of faith and believe that God is bigger than any statistic and that He still has the power to rebuild what is broken and restore what is lost between men and women today.

In the following pages, you will find true love stories filled with hope and humor that will inspire you to make challenging life-changing choices. Each chapter also contains real-life love coaching, powerful prayers, inspiring scriptural love letters to draw you to the heart of God, and a Treasure of Truth to hang on to when you feel like giving up. If you're reading the book in a group, you will find two questions at the end of each chapter that should lead to some interesting discussion. There is also a QR code there, which will lead you to a video where I answer some of the hardest questions about love, men, and marriage. You can view the clips from a smart phone or online.

I am praying that this teaching and truth will bring real change, refreshment, and some relief from the heaviness and heartache we women carry every day. When we finish our time together, may our lives give us and the world a second chance to see what real faith and true love look like when lived out with a "legacy perspective."

In His Love,
Sheri Rose

Special note: This book can also be an amazing resource for a seven-week small group study in your home or at church. Simply read two chapters a week and watch my seven-week teaching series, either online or from a DVD, which is designed to allow me to help you lead your group.

SMALL GROUP GUIDE

THIS BOOK IS a stand-alone resource for all readers, but if you feel led to facilitate a small group in your home or church, below are some guidelines to ensure a successful and meaningful experience.

1. As women enter, consider having worship music playing, because it will set a peaceful tone in the room.
2. The ideal size of a small group is six to seven women. If you're planning to do this with a large group of women, divide them into these smaller-sized groups and choose a discussion leader for each table.
3. Be sure to let your group know you are hosting the group, but you are not a professional counselor. You are not responsible for solving everyone's relationship issues. As questions arise, if you don't know the answer, look to God's Word and let the group know you'll get back to them.

4. Don't let yourself or others give advice outside of biblical guidelines.

5. Address the issue of covering your men and not oversharing. Attendees should avoid humiliating the men in their lives by revealing too much.

6. Let women know they should each keep their responses to questions of no more than three or four minutes each, so everyone has an opportunity to share.

7. At the end of each group session, spend time praying for each other's concerns and relational challenges.

8. Use the outline/recap of each chapter, which begins on page 193, as a reference to upcoming topics.

9. If you are planning on serving refreshments, arrange to have people alternate bringing snacks and drinks each week.

10. Feel free to make a copy of this guide and distribute it to everyone in your group.

Consider letting Sheri Rose lead your group using the companion *Your Heart's Desire* DVD, which includes a seven-week Bible study series, coming out in fall 2012. If you'd like to find out more about Sheri Rose and her teaching ministry, visit www.biblelifecoaching.com.

1

DESIRING A "HAPPILY EVER AFTER"

*Fighting the Temptation to
Give Up on Love and Marriage*

⁓

*Love never gives up, never loses faith, is always hopeful,
and endures through every circumstance.*

1 CORINTHIANS 13:7

I BELIEVE WHEN a man walks down the aisle and says "I do," his every hope and intention is that his marriage will be for life. He sincerely desires to understand and take care of the beloved bride he has chosen. He romanced her and worked hard to express his love so she would want to spend the rest of her life with him. He was determined to be her hero and lovingly lead her safely through life. The challenge for each man begins after the "I dos" because generally no one has taught him how to accomplish his God-appointed position in a woman's life.

Eventually, a man's attempts at love, leadership, and even heroism may miss their mark, and his beloved bride gradually withdraws emotionally from the very one she hoped would give her happily ever after. Sadly, she often closes up her spirit in order to protect her heart from any more hurt.

The man she longs for ends up feeling frustrated and angry at himself, and he may give up trying. Their love story, which once fostered hopes of intimacy, happiness, and growing old together, withers into isolation, pain, and despair—sometimes even divorce. That was certainly what I saw growing up.

I was raised in a non-Christian home. My parents have each been married and divorced to three different people, so as part of several blended families, it was hard for me to understand what a healthy family is supposed to be. Needless to say, when I was growing up all I understood about marriage was "unhappily ever after." So my heart's desire was to find a godly man to love me forever and then to live with him in a lovely home with a white picket fence. To be honest, that white picket fence was almost as important as the man because somehow the fence represented the foundation of a stable family that I never had as a child and protection from heartbreak.

I gave my heart to the Lord at age twenty-four and fell madly in love with Jesus. A few years later, I met and married my husband, Steve, and we became the parents to a son, Jacob, and eleven years later to our daughter, Emily. Because of my love for God and my husband, I honestly didn't think anything could shake my faith. Then in the summer of 2007, my happily ever after was wiped out and my faith was tested when all I feared about marriage became reality. All that I had known to be true appeared to be a false hope. The foundation I had worked so hard to build and protect was almost destroyed, along with my ministry, in that season of my life. I truly believed that God had forsaken me.

I had just finished writing my book *Preparing Him for the Other Woman: A Mother's Guide to Raising Her Son to Love a Wife and Lead a Family.* It was one of the most difficult books I've ever written, but finally I had completed it and was ready to send it to the publisher. However, as I excitedly ran upstairs to my office to send the manuscript, I suddenly felt as if something dark hovered over me. My passion was drowned out by the fear of an attack from the enemy that could come against me and my family if I stepped on his territory . . . young men and their future marriages.

The reality hit me. I was putting a book out there that would shine some light in the darkness. After all, the devil has used many of his tools to destroy our young boys and confuse them about who they are and what their role is in a woman's life. I did not think I was strong enough to handle what could come if I stood in front of the giants in the land that were killing the confidence of our young men. I called the publisher and said I'd need to wait and pray for courage before submitting the manuscript.

I went to my husband and my son, who was eighteen years old and a senior in high school at the time. I told them of my fears and asked if they would stand by me no matter what happened. Then I looked at Jake and asked him if he had any plans of rebelling against his faith once he graduated from high school. I told him I was willing to give him freedom to find his own faith in Christ, but I didn't want to put out a book about raising boys if my own son was going to walk away from the Lord. He reassured me that he was strong in his faith and that he felt I should publish the book. Three days later I decided to take the chance to make a difference and sent in the manuscript.

Several months later the book began climbing the charts, and everything seemed to be going well. I even began speaking with my son at conferences for mothers of boys. Then three months into my book tour, my fear of attack became reality. My husband had taken a job that we had both prayed for. This job appeared to be a blessing and gave him the opportunity to do what he loved. After he'd spent so many years working alongside me in my ministry, I looked forward to supporting him in his desired career.

Yet his new position required him to violate some of the boundaries we had put in place to protect our marriage, such as always attending evening social engagements together. While my heart was troubled by the compromises he had to make, Steve didn't see the dangers. He loved me and our kids, and he thought the boundaries, which we'd agreed on early in our marriage, were no longer necessary now that our marriage was strong.

Like many wives, I sensed that other women were coming after my man before my husband did. They were mostly attracted by how much he loved me. They wanted that kind of love. Because my husband was not the one pursuing any woman, he thought he was safe. Sadly, we ended up separated. There I was in the public eye of ministry, fighting to save future marriages, and somehow my own marriage was falling apart.

My son was devastated by the division between his mom and dad. It was too hard for him to deal with all his confusion, pain, and anger. He was upset to see me unable to get control of my emotions and expressing doubts about my faith for the first time. Once Steve and I were living apart, he also felt pressured to become the "man of the house." In despair, Jacob eventually took a break from his faith and began using drugs and alcohol to comfort himself.

Meanwhile, I hit the lowest point in my faith journey. Because of the upheaval in my home growing up, I had been through many horrible experiences. Yet when I rebuilt my broken life on Christ as a young adult, I assumed my life would never crumble again. I had been taught to run to God for cover when there was a great attack, but now I felt like He had left me alone on the battlefield to fight for myself. It appeared that all I had believed about God and all my effort to build a strong foundation for my own family had been shattered. My pain, my shame, and my life were an embarrassment. I felt as if I were battling an out-of-control fire that would burn up everything I loved and lived for.

Even worse was my fear of how this division between Steve and me would affect our seven-year-old daughter, Emily. I spent so many nights holding her while she cried and asked, "What happened to our family and why aren't we all living together anymore?" One night she asked, "Does God really answer prayer?" How I longed during that time for an answer that would increase her faith, but for the first time I had lost mine.

It's hard when you're in the middle of a war to find your peace or your purpose for fighting. I had thought I was fighting to further God's Kingdom on earth by equipping mothers to raise warriors, but it appeared I had lost the fight in my own life.

I moved in with a precious friend of mine who had a daughter Emily's age, and we lived in their guest room for most of the summer. Every night I would cry out to God as I questioned why He had not protected me while I was attempting to accomplish something for His glory. What I didn't know was that He was actually going to use this trial to unlock me from a greater fear and to free me from holding on so tightly to my family.

After weeks of anguish, I cried out, "How can I get through this and find a new foundation to build on?" It was in that moment I felt like the Lord asked me a bigger question: *Was My life given on a cross for you not enough for you to finish strong even if it means surrendering the life you wanted?*

For the first time I realized that my heart's true desire was to feel loved and secure, and yet no man on earth could love me the way my Lord does. It was in that moment of crisis that

I found the true meaning of following Christ. God had not forsaken me, but He had wanted to free me from depending on others to give me my happily ever after.

That night I gave my deepest heart's desire to God and chose to follow Him at any cost. In exchange, He gave me something so much better than a white picket fence. He surrounded me with His presence and gave me peace that was stronger than my circumstances. My faith was no longer in people; it was in Christ alone. Although nothing outwardly had changed yet, I had been changed. I woke up the next morning and let Steve and Jake know that I loved them, and no matter how our family worked out, I was going to finish the work that God had given me. Steve and I were sobered by the realization that we were in danger of throwing away everything we had built. Restoring our marriage, however, was excruciatingly painful and more difficult than either of us expected. For three years, we had to work through our anger and lay down our hurts for the greater good of our marriage. Even with intensive counseling, we separated and reunited a few more times as we dealt with the deep wounds we had inflicted on one another.

By God's grace, Jake eventually showed up at my door and chose to give his life 100 percent to God. He went to Los Angeles to be in full-time ministry and work on the streets with the Los Angeles Dream Center.

The ultimate payoff came when Steve and I attended our son's wedding together. We couldn't help but think how different the day would have been had we not fought for our own marriage and for the legacy we would pass on to our two children. Jacob and Amanda's wedding not only marked the beginning of their life together, it also was the day Steve and I realized how much our marriage truly meant to us and others.

Today the foundation of our marriage is stronger than ever. Of course, there are still the challenges that come in every marriage, but we remain standing and have chosen to finish our lives together, for better or for worse, in times of trouble and times of joy, in times of sickness and times of health, until death do us part. Steve and I delight to watch our son and his wife work together to raise their new baby girl, Olive True, in the ways of the Lord.

As I think back on my own journey out of utter despair, I realize that even if reconciliation with Steve hadn't been possible, God would have enabled me to live out my faith with the right attitude so I could pass on a legacy of hope and joy to my children. As hard as this trial was, it taught me a valuable lesson: life may never become what we want it to be, but if we are committed to live driven by eternity, everything we do will become a reflection of God's grace and glory.

How tragic it would have been if I had walked away from all those years of ministry because of the actions of man. You may be thinking, *Sheri Rose, you have no idea what I have been through.* You're right—I don't and I never want to underestimate anyone's pain. Yet I believe the chapters to come will bring healing for your heart.

Let's take a moment and think about all the hardships so many of us have endured. It would be tragic to waste the painful places we have walked. We can use our mistakes to make us wiser and our pain to make us passionate about devoting our lives to a purpose greater than our own personal happiness.

We can think about it this way: even if we have lost all faith in all men or the men we once loved, we shouldn't lose faith in our Lord, who loved us so much He gave His life for us on a cross and who longs to meet our deepest heart's desire . . . to be loved and to give love!

LOVE COACHING

I don't know where you stand today with the man you love or loved—or if you are single, divorced, separated, or widowed—but would you consider taking a step of faith with me and begin building a new foundation of love? I have discovered that healing begins and hope is restored when you and I use our pain to bring change and allow God to show us a picture bigger than our own desires.

❧ *Build from the wreckage . . .*

Some of you will rebuild the deserted ruins of your cities. Then you will be known as a rebuilder of walls and a restorer of homes.
ISAIAH 58:12

Your heavenly Father knows how hard it is to find the strength to pour love and forgiveness into someone who has caused you pain. He hurts with you, and He knows that when you and I are weak, we may have no idea where to find a fresh start. That is why we need a Savior. He is the author of a new beginning.

Regardless of the relational devastation you face, no one can keep you from finishing strong for God's glory. The way you fight and face your personal battles will become your mission statement. Look at what you can do for the sake of society and your children's future. Fight your feelings and work toward a future that will bring some relief and refreshment to this world. It is your life and it's your time. Do whatever you can to build a new foundation.

Even if there is no chance for reconciliation, don't add to the wreckage by giving in to despair. I know it is hard to believe one person's love and reaction to the ruins of relationships will help rebuild our broken society, but it's true. If you are unable to take the right action, pray hard and ask God to give you a right heart and attitude. If you have children, stand with honor for their sake and continue to pray that your man will step into his God-appointed position to become the man he was created to be. If you're single and see any marriage struggling, I encourage you to pray for that marriage because your prayer will be a part of the rebuilding of that marriage.

Our God can and will rebuild a beautiful life out of any broken heart willing to make a change. He will use one sacrificial choice, one act of forgiveness, one sincere repentant heart, and one woman who is willing to step out in faith and start rebuilding with love.

🌿 Rebuild with your words . . .

The words of the godly are a life-giving fountain.
PROVERBS 10:11

My son, Jake, has always been an excellent communicator and very relational. When he was eleven, I asked him an interesting marriage question. "Jake, how can I be a better wife to your dad?"

Without missing a beat, he replied, "Mom, you need to say fewer words and say nicer things to Daddy."

I thought, *Wow, what wisdom coming from the mouth of a young boy who has never been married.*

God says our words can become a life-giving fountain. Have you ever noticed how rough stones can become beautiful when caressed by the gentle, consistent force of water running over them? Without water, they appear lifeless and rough. But in a gentle stream, even jagged corners are softened and sparkle with life. Our words can be just like that spring of water. Today I realize the Scripture is true: the power of life and death really is in our tongue (Proverbs 18:21).

I wish I could take back some of the things I said about Steve in front of Jacob during the worst days of our marriage. I now see how I allowed my frustrations to become a part of me instead of understanding that my anger and harsh words made me part of the problem. Even though everything I was saying to my husband was how I truthfully felt, it wasn't fixing the problem or watering anyone around me.

I let my words increase the tension and tear down my family foundation without even realizing it. I had justified my actions by nurturing the disappointments I felt toward my husband, and gradually my daily words and my heart became stone-cold toward him. The truth is that what we feel eventually comes out in our words and then our actions. If we are not careful, the actions we take when we are hurting will eventually become our legacy.

LET US PRAY

Dear God,

I need Your power and grace to love the one who has hurt me. I confess I am angry and overwhelmed by the way things turned out. I invite You now to turn my heart toward heaven so I might live out the rest of my life for the greater cause of bringing glory to Your name. Help me leave a legacy of unconditional love. In Jesus' name I pray, amen.

I lift up my eyes to the mountains—
*   where does my help come from?*
My help comes from the LORD,
*   the Maker of heaven and earth.*

PSALM 121:1-2, NIV

His Love Letter to You

My Beloved Daughter,

I want to birth a new thing in your heart and bring forth the perfect peace and plan I have for you. I am asking you as your heavenly Father to look to the future and not to the past to find the path I have prepared for you.

I know it won't be easy, but it will be worth letting go of what once was to receive all I have for you. Your past has prepared you for your purpose, and nothing and no one can stop My plans for your life. Don't allow disappointment to direct your path. Now is the time to take My hand and walk out the rest of your days on earth with Me . . . your heavenly Daddy.

Love,
Your Creator of new life!

For I am about to do something new. See, I have already begun! Do you not see it? I will make a pathway through the wilderness. I will create rivers in the dry wasteland.

ISAIAH 43:19

TREASURE OF TRUTH

REAL CHANGE HAPPENS WHEN WE BEGIN THE
CHANGE WE LONG TO SEE.

Love Questions for Your Small Group

1. What is your heart's desire for your relationship with a man?

2. Do you ever feel that God is letting you down in your key relationships? If so, how do you deal with your doubt and confusion?

3. Ask one another, "How can we pray for a man in your life?" Then set aside time to bring your requests and as a group lift up your men before the Lord.

Love Question Online with Sheri Rose

 What if my husband has no desire to rebuild?

Snap the code with your smartphone or visit the link for Sheri Rose's insights.

www.tyndal.es/YourHeartsDesire1

FOR MORE TEACHING VIDEOS FROM SHERI ROSE,
GO TO WWW.BIBLELIFECOACHING.COM.

2

DESIRING A GODLY MAN TO MARRY (FOR SINGLES)

Fighting NOT to Settle for Less than God's Best for Me

The LORD directs the steps of the godly.
He delights in every detail of their lives.

PSALM 37:23

IF YOU ARE SINGLE, I know it can be hard to keep hoping you'll find a man who will sweep you off your feet and then fight to protect his family and his marriage. That's especially true if you haven't seen this type of love modeled.

My own dad, whom I loved dearly, longed to rescue his family but did not know how. Though I'd become used to hearing my parents scream at one another, I'll never forget one particular night when I was eleven. My dad came into my room after another loud fight with my mom. I saw the fear on his face and the tears in his eyes as he knelt by my bed to tell me he was moving out. My parents divorced shortly after. The tragedy of their love story was that my dad wanted to make his marriage work, yet eventually he felt so hopeless he gave up. No matter how much my parents fought, though, deep down my dad longed to be a hero and my mom longed to be rescued.

My heart's desire wasn't all that different from my mom's. Even though my parents' divorce made me cautious about marriage, I still wanted to marry a man who would cherish me and love me unconditionally. As a lonely, overweight, drug-using teen, however, I wasn't considered a hot prospect by guys my age. In fact, my school's Homecoming king dubbed me "Sheri the Whale"!

So I lost over fifty pounds in an effort to get a man to love me. And my weight became my worth. When the weight came off and I became clean of drugs, things changed. For the first time, I got the attention I craved from men. At age twenty-four, I became a Christian and was so excited about my new life with Jesus. I finally felt truly loved. Still, my longing to find a flesh-and-blood hero hadn't gone away. I publicly testified to the change Christ had made in my life; however, I wasn't quite ready to give up control of my mission to find a godly man. For some reason, I thought God needed my help.

Like many young women, I daydreamed about the day I would become engaged and tried to picture what that storybook moment might look like. Would my future fiancé, aware of how important my faith was to me, quietly ask me to become his bride as we sat together in church? Would he take me out for a romantic dinner and surprise me with a beautiful diamond ring while declaring I was the only woman he had ever loved? Or, given that women had come a long way, baby, might I be the one to pop the question? My dreaming became reality as I lived out all three scenarios within a couple of weeks.

Now, I realize I'm not the only woman who has been engaged to more than one man or whose fiancé called off the nuptials. I'm guessing, though, that I'm the only woman you've heard of who was engaged to multiple men at the same time—and who drove them all away in a single night.

Before you judge me too harshly, let me explain. For starters, though I knew I wanted to marry a man who loved the Lord like I did, I never bothered to ask God to help me find a godly man. Instead, I tried to help Him out by dating every Christian guy I was attracted to. Because I traveled to many different cities during the year for my job, I was able to find potential husbands in many of the cities and churches I visited while on the road.

It seemed harmless and innocent for a while, but then I began feeling overwhelmed by my love addiction. Without even realizing it, my Lord was no longer the love of my life; He had been replaced with my obsession to find a man. Eventually, I became especially close to three good, godly men. Sadly, my lack of wisdom and trust in God ended up wiping out everyone's happily ever after. Although each of these men knew about the others, they did *not* know they had all proposed to me within the same week. Nor did they know that the girl they loved was a wimp who did not have the courage to say no to any of them out of fear of hurting them or losing them. Now if you're ready for a good laugh and a good life lesson, read on to find out how this love adventure actually played out and what happened when I was busted by all three of them at the same time.

First there was Michael, a model who lived in Phoenix. He was the most fun and romantic of the three. However, he wasn't a Christian, so I did what I called "missionary dating" (FYI: it's a dangerous thing to do). He was also four years younger than I was. I really liked him but knew I had to give him up, so with a heavy heart I broke up with him. A few weeks after our breakup, he called to tell me he had become a Christian and asked me to come celebrate his newfound faith with him at his church, where he was getting baptized. I couldn't help but wonder if God was giving me back something I had given up for Him. Not long after, we agreed to get back together, though I'd made it clear I'd continue seeing other people.

One evening when Michael and I went to church together, he pulled out a ring and proposed. I was shocked. Maybe this is a sign that he's the one, I told myself. He'd proposed to me in church, after all.

So I said yes. I know now that my decision was based purely on emotion—not on faith or logic. When my dad warned me against marrying Michael, I stood firm. "Remember when you and Mom were going to get married, and everyone tried to talk you out of it?" I asked him. "You didn't listen. You did what you thought was right."

"Yeah, and look how that turned out," he shot back. "Will

Michael be able to lead you through this life? Don't forget he's much younger than you and is new in his faith."

About the time my dad accepted the idea that I would marry Michael without his blessing (another FYI: it's generally not a good idea to marry a man your parents don't approve of), my father's warning stayed in my head and I started feeling anxious and afraid. Would Michael really be able to meet my heart's desires? What if I had made the wrong choice?

Then David, a chiropractor from San Diego I had been dating, called and invited me to dinner. We set the date, and once we were seated in the restaurant, I tried to find the right moment to tell him I was now engaged to someone else, but David was at his most charming and didn't make it easy.

I also couldn't help comparing Michael to David, a mature, reliable professional. I longed for security, something I wasn't sure Michael could give me. After ordering dinner, David reached into his pocket and did something completely unexpected. He pulled out an engagement ring and passionately said, "I love you, Sheri. I want to spend every day with you for the rest of my life. Will you marry me?"

My head was spinning. "I've never told that to anyone before in my life," he continued, "because I only wanted to say 'I love you' to one person."

I melted. Was this God's way of rescuing me from the wrong person? So I said yes, leaving out the tiny detail that I had already agreed to marry another man.

Now that I was engaged to two men at the same time, I prayed and puzzled over the situation without finding a solution out of my mess. My heart's desire was to find one man to marry—not two!

I was out of control and did not know what to say, so I disappeared and dodged both Michael's and David's calls. To get away from the stress and figure out what to do, I asked my friend Kyman, a carpenter in San Jose whose missionary grandparents had helped lead me to Jesus, if I could visit. He had always accepted me unconditionally, and because there wasn't much "electricity" in our relationship, I figured he was the safe friend I needed right then. (Of course, what I really needed was a therapist to help me untangle the mess I had made!)

I spent a blessedly relaxing week with Kyman and his grandparents. Because I never mentioned my dilemma and simply enjoyed going to the beach and having long conversations with Kyman, I was free of stress for the first time in ages. I never wanted our time together to end.

That led to my next impetuous move. One day out of the blue I said, "Kyman, let me ask you something. If I said I wanted to marry you, would you want to marry me?" I wasn't actually asking, of course; I was speaking hypothetically. Kyman missed the nuance entirely.

"Oh yes, Sheri," he said, his eyes welling with tears. "Yes."

Kyman was so easygoing and helpful. We never fought, and I loved his grandparents. This had to be it! I decided, forgetting the two other "its" in the equation for the moment.

Now I had to figure out how to tell both Michael and David that I was going to marry Kyman. More confused than ever, I realized I had to go back to work and produce a talent showcase in San Francisco. Not only did I not want to lose my job, I needed a diversion. My best friend, Joyce, worked with me, so I assigned her to handle the multiple phone calls from Michael, David, and Kyman, all of whom wanted to discuss our future wedding plans.

Eventually, though, each guy called my dad's office on his own and was able to convince my dad to tell him where I was. As they began calling me at the hotel, I continued stalling for time, telling them I was overwhelmed and scared of making the same mistake my parents had made.

They all asked to see me. "No," I told them. "I need more time to figure this out."

The talent showcase went smoothly, and finally the closing program arrived. At the end of the evening, the winning contestants would be announced. Just before the curtain went up, I offered to pray with any of the contestants who wanted me to do so. Several did, and I had just finished praying for them when Joyce walked over to me with a strange look.

"You'll have to get down on your knees for this one," she whispered. "Maybe even try fasting—or running really fast."

"What are you talking about?" I asked.

She led me to the curtain, opened it a tiny slit, and told me to look to the right at the front row. As the house lights started to dim, I looked where she was pointing and thought I'd die. Sitting side by side were Michael, David, and Kyman—my three fiancés—total strangers to each other, each with roses in his hands.

Just then the house lights were turned off. The music cue

came. I had no choice but to start the show. It was definitely not one of my better performances. My hands were sweating. I mispronounced the names of contestants and sponsors. I missed some cues and forgot to give others. I was so desperate I almost wished I'd have a heart attack so I wouldn't have to face my three fiancés!

As the winners received their final applause, I looked down at the front row to see all three men still smiling—thank heaven. But at that very moment, I saw Michael turn to the other two and say, "Isn't she awesome? That's the girl I'm going to marry." The smiles vanished as they began talking.

While I was still onstage, David shot me an angry look and stormed out. Michael quickly approached me as soon as he saw me enter the auditorium, while Kyman waited patiently in a corner.

I came clean to Michael and then to Kyman. "I'm so sorry. I never meant to hurt you, but I realize I can't marry anybody right now. And trust me, you don't want to marry me." Later that evening I left a message on David's voice mail. As cold as that sounds, I wanted him to hear my apology as soon as possible.

Late that night, I had to face some difficult questions. How could I have hurt three wonderful men this way? Why wasn't I able to be honest with them before something like this happened? Then the real question: why hadn't I trusted the Lord to guide me in my relationships?

I had gone through the motions of praying for God to lead me to the right man, but I had resisted turning everything over to Him. God had my attention now. I finally decided to stop my search for "Mr. Right" and get my heart right with God so He could direct my path.

I don't believe our desire to find a good man is wrong, and we do have every reason to be cautious. Even in the church it seems that just about every day we hear about another man of faith who has fallen away from his wife, his family, and his moral convictions. Single women tell me about the heartache they experience after years of dating men who seem unwilling to commit to a family; others talk about how they feel overlooked by men who seem more interested in enjoying eye candy than in finding a soul mate.

Yet as I discovered on the night I finally had to face Michael, David, and Kyman, deception, mistrust, and pain are real dangers if we haven't lost ourselves in Christ's love before we give our heart to a man. (FYI: all three of my former fiancés attended my wedding just to witness me actually saying "I do.") God Himself reminds us to love Him with all our heart, all our soul, all our strength, and all our mind (see Luke 10:27). Why? Not only will this glorify Him, God knows that He alone can meet our deepest heart's desire.

Our love relationship with the Lord will anchor us. We will not be moved when we know that Christ is our Rock, our Knight in shining armor, the one we've been looking for.

When we love Him with all our heart, we will be less desperate for men's love and more delighted by His.

No one is more beautiful than the woman who loves God with all of her heart and then freely gives that love to others. A woman who truly is in love with God becomes irresistibly beautiful.

LOVE COACHING

If you are single, don't hesitate to cry out to God on the days when you long for a man. Just don't forget to rest and rejoice in His love, knowing that the Lord will direct your steps and that He delights in every detail of your life. In my case, fiancé #1 (Michael) was actually the instrument God used to introduce me to the man He had for me. Ironically, Steve, my husband, was the one who had led Michael to the Lord. It's funny for me to think of the creative ways God works: He used my husband to lead Michael to Himself and He used Michael to lead me to the husband my heart desired.

Review the list . . .

My precious single friends, I want to give you a "love checklist" to help you avoid pouring your heart into the wrong relationship. Trust me: it is better to be single and satisfied than heartbroken in the wrong relationship.

The wise woman's love checklist

1. Look at the way a man loves his mother, because it is the way he will eventually love his wife.
2. Pay attention to the way he reacts when there is stress or conflict.
3. Meet his friends and keep in mind that the people he hangs with are a reflection of his heart.
4. Pay attention to what your good friends see in him, because often those who love you can see better than you can see when you're falling in love.
5. Look at what he reads and what he watches on television, because they will be a reflection of his moral fiber.
6. Do your best not to be too physical, because it will cloud your vision and confuse your heart.
7. It is imperative that a man respect your boundaries without challenging them.
8. Ask him to pray for you often, because you will need a man who knows how to cover you in prayer.
9. Ask yourself whether you feel at home when you're with him or whether you act like someone you're not to get him to like you.
10. Before you say "I do," go through premarital counseling with a pastor.

LET US PRAY

Dear Lord,

I pray for my future husband, wherever he is in the world right now. Prepare me to become the kind of bride he will need when we come together. Until You make me ready for him, let the only intimate relationship I seek be with You. Blind my eyes from wanting any other man than the one You have for me. Remove all men in my life who may keep me from recognizing him. Give me wisdom to seek what is pure and right in Your sight while I wait for him. Put such a deep passion in my heart for my purpose that I won't be distracted or discouraged from pursuing all that You have for me.

Deliver me from the traps of the enemy, and train me now to resist temptation. Keep me from falling into a counterfeit relationship, and give me the strength not to settle for second best. Give me the stamina to run this "singles" race until I cross the finish line and receive his heart—and Your blessing—as the prize. Amen.

Trust in the Lord with all your heart; do not depend on your own understanding. Seek his will in all you do, and he will show you which path to take.

PROVERBS 3:5-6

His Love Letter to You

My Beloved Bride,

I want to be the Love of your life. I am the Giver of every good gift, and I see your need to be loved by a man, but I want to be your first love and I want your heart to be committed totally to Me. If you will settle into Me first, you will be able to love a man the way I created you to love. What must I do to prove My love for you? Can I send another cool breeze on a hot summer day? Can I set more stars in the sky to remind you of My heavenly love for you? Can I provide for another need to prove I will take care of you? I love you with an everlasting love, and one day we will see each other face-to-face. On that day you will see that you are, and always have been, My treasured bride.

Love,
Your Lord and true Prince

For your royal husband delights in your beauty;
honor him, for he is your lord.

PSALM 45:11

. . . .

TREASURE OF TRUTH

YOU DO NOT NEED A MAN TO PUSH THE "PLAY BUTTON" FOR YOUR LIFE TO BEGIN.

Love Questions for Your Small Group

1. What lessons did Sheri Rose learn from her triple engagement?
   What did you learn from her FYIs in the story?

2. What do you think of the wise woman's love checklist under Love
   Coaching on page 25?

Love Question Online with Sheri Rose

Is there only one man God has selected for me? If so,
what if I missed him?

Snap the code with your smartphone or visit the link for Sheri Rose's insights.
www.tyndal.es/YourHeartsDesire2

FOR MORE TEACHING VIDEOS FROM SHERI ROSE,
GO TO WWW.BIBLELIFECOACHING.COM.

3

DESIRING TO LEAVE A LEGACY FOR MY LOVED ONES

Fighting to Give an Everlasting Blessing to My Broken Family

~~~~~~⁓

I have fought the good fight, I have finished the race,
I have kept the faith. Now there is in store for me the crown.

2 TIMOTHY 4:7-8, NIV

I USED TO FEEL God owed me a "happily ever after" as an adult because of all I had to endure as a child. I was convinced that the only way I could glorify God with my life was if I had all the things that made my family and me appear blessed and favored. As you know, life and love rarely turn out like we want them to, and God does not need to make us comfortable to make Himself look good.

The truth is our Savior's first bed was a manger. It was nothing fancy and was surrounded by dirty animals. Then He left this world with a very broken body, and when He died on the cross, it looked as if His life had been a waste. However, His death was not the end. It was the beginning of a forever life for you and me.

Our lives may not be the ones we have longed for, but the greatest testimony is not how we started but how we finish. It isn't getting what we want; it's giving what we have. It isn't getting our way; it's doing God's will no matter what anyone else we love does. The legacy is not in our comfort; it is in our character.

I know this is easier said than lived out.

Is it even possible to fight the temptation to give up, and instead finish strong, when you are a woman who has dedicated your life to loving, encouraging, praying for, and pouring yourself into your husband, only to watch him, in a moment of weakness, destroy the foundation you worked so hard to build and leave your family in ruins? As hard as it is to keep believing when you're in the middle of a battle like that, the answer to this question is . . . yes!

I invite you to read a real-life love story that I believe will give you the passion you may need to persevere under any and every trial. It will also give you a true picture of what love looks like when lived out with a legacy perspective. I call this story "The Grand Finale."

John and Marie were college sweethearts who dreamed of furthering God's Kingdom together. During the first decade of their ministry, God blessed them with a growing church, two beautiful children, and a strong and loving marriage. Because of their commitment to God and one another, they became one of the most respected couples in the community. Their marriage was a beacon of hope to other young couples who wondered what marriage could be. John loved the ministry, and he loved the life God had given him. He was passionate about the call of God on his life, and he truly loved his wife.

One day as John was busy working at the church, a young lady burst through the door of the church office. She was crying hysterically, and John came out of his office to see what he might do to help. As she struggled to catch her breath, she told John about her desperate attempts to escape from her abusive husband. She was sure he would kill her if he found her, but she didn't feel safe going to the police because they had failed to help her in the past. John quickly called Marie and asked her to take the young lady to a safe place. After Marie helped this distraught young mom gather her kids and some clothes, she brought them home to spend the night with her and John.

In a matter of days, Marie and John's love for this young woman led her to become a Christian. After spending a few weeks in their home, she seemed like a new person. She was hungry for God and at peace. John and Marie felt great, knowing they had made such an impact on this young woman and her kids.

When this woman and her children were still staying in John and Marie's home several weeks later, many of his good friends and family approached John and recommended that the woman find housing with another single mom. He was blinded, saying, "Marie is really helping her. I can't ask her to leave now; she may fall away from the Lord."

John's good intentions without wisdom and his unwillingness to heed the warnings of others left him unguarded against the enemy's attack. One night when Marie was out leading a Bible study, John was home alone with the woman. She had fallen for Marie's husband and was determined to have him for herself. Tragically, Marie walked into her home to find John and the young woman in their bed together. Everything John and Marie had built was destroyed.

Unable to handle his guilt, John felt like such a failure that he left his marriage, his children, and his church to marry this young, attractive woman. Two years into his new marriage, however, he was diagnosed with acute leukemia and was given only ten weeks to live. His second wife, who was still in her early twenties, decided she did not want to take care of a dying man. After emptying his bank account, she left him alone to die. He had no family and no loving church body to rally around him. In fact, he had nothing to show for his years of hard work and dedication to ministry.

As tragic as this story is, the ending is proof of God's amazing grace. Marie decided that when John died, he should be free of guilt and shame. She went to his bedside, not gloating with condemnation, but offering to care for and forgive him. Her kids seemed almost angry at her for loving her ex-husband after all he had done. Her friends from church asked her why she was helping him. However, Marie wanted her children and church to remember not how John had left them, but how she took care of him, never leaving his bedside until he drew his last breath.

On the day John died, his children and members from his church gathered around his bedside with Marie. They held hands and shared memories of how John had touched others' lives when he was walking with God. Marie got a greater gift. By her sacrifice, she began the healing in her own heart and in her children's hearts. Today they can all live free of regret and anger because they said a final good-bye to their father in a setting of God's glorious love.

Marie sets an example for all of us women who have been hurt. Yes, we might feel some relief from seeing those who have caused us pain get what they deserve. But in the eternal view of things, the greater healing takes place by loving people the most when they deserve it the least, the way that God loves us.

Marie gave John an amazing final gift: she gave him her forgiveness and the opportunity to finish what he had started, even if it had to take place on his deathbed after their marriage had ended.

Yes, God hates divorce, and yes, He knows the pain of adultery is so great that He actually allows us to divorce if our man is unfaithful. But when there is any possibility that our marriages can be saved, we need to look at the bigger picture and fight the temptation to give up. Even if there is nothing to be saved, we can ask God to help heal our hurt, and we can avoid talking about our current or former husband or marriage with our children or with others outside of a counseling situation. The only way to get past the devastation of unfaithfulness is to keep our eyes fixed on our faithful God, knowing He will not waste this pain. Furthermore, the sin of another person, even our own husband's, cannot stop God's purposes from being fulfilled in our lives or our children's lives.

If we want to finish strong, we will have to let go of this life and live driven by eternity. No one will ever remember how comfortable we were, but they will definitely remember if we had courageous faith and unconditional love. We can believe that God does have a legacy for us and that we will find it when we cry out to Him and ask Him to process this pain in us in a way that will leave a legacy of real love.

LOVE COACHING

❧ *Use your brokenness . . .*

[Love] always protects, always trusts, always hopes, always perseveres.
1 CORINTHIANS 13:7, NIV

I know what it's like to be so broken that it is hard to believe that the painful place we're walking in could lead to anything good. One of the ways I have found healing when I'm hurting is to take my need to be loved and pour that love into others so my pain can be used to glorify the Lord. The most valuable things you and I have to give are free— forgiveness, a word of encouragement, a prayer offered up for someone, a hug, a deed that helps someone in need and shows we care.

I know it's hard to give when we are hurting, but when it's all said and done and this life is over, all that will remain is our love and our legacy. How we face and finish our battles will define who we are in Christ. There are a lot of reasons to give up, but there are greater reasons to finish strong. In the middle of the fire it may feel like we'll never get out, but once the flames die down, we will find ourselves closer to God and purified from the fire. We are here on earth for only a little while, but we're going to celebrate the lives we lived on earth for all eternity.

❧ Stay in church . . .

But if we are living in the light, as God is in the light, then we have fellowship with each other, and the blood of Jesus, his Son, cleanses us from all sin.
1 JOHN 1:7

Although it may be difficult to remain in church if your husband has humiliated you by his actions, that is exactly where you need to be when your world is falling apart. And if you have children, keep your kids in church. Remember, it is your husband who has been unfaithful to you, not God. When your world has shattered, you need to surround yourself with the family of God and let those who love you pray over you and stand in the gap for you. *Note*: If your church is too painful a reminder of your situation, then find a new church with a support group, but stay in God's house when you're hurting.

🌿 *Stand . . .*

So, my dear brothers and sisters, be strong and immovable. Always work enthusiastically for the Lord, for you know that nothing you do for the Lord is ever useless.

1 CORINTHIANS 15:58

When you have no idea what to do and you're too weak to fight the good fight, just be still and know He is God. Let Him fight for you. All you need to do is stand. What I mean by "stand" is to avoid making any decisions while you're in the heat of emotion. Instead, take time to seek wise counsel and to allow your heart to calm down. Stand; don't walk away. Hide under His wings and let Him walk you through this. Once the crisis has passed, I promise you'll still be standing in His strength.

🌿 *Protect your home . . .*

Commit yourselves wholeheartedly to these words of mine. . . . Teach them to your children. Talk about them when you are at home and when you are on the road, when you are going to bed and when you are getting up. Write them on the doorposts of your house.

DEUTERONOMY 11:18-20

Our homes need to be places of protection and places for us to raise up our families in the way of the Lord. If we invite trouble into our homes, we're putting our families and ourselves at risk. Of course, many Christians have the best of intentions, longing to reach people for Christ, when they invite people into their homes. I love outreach, but it's important that we reach out to others in their environment and not bring them into our environment—our personal homes. There have been countless stories of children molested in their own homes because of who has been allowed to enter. Many marriages have been taken down because a man or woman who was in a couple's home was not pure of heart.

❧ Write your mission statement . . .

I have fought the good fight, I have finished the race, and I have remained faithful.
2 TIMOTHY 4:7

One of the best ways to finish strong is to write somewhere in the front of your Bible what you want to be remembered for and what you want your mission statement to be. Write a list of things that will help you leave that legacy for your children and those you love. It will be a wonderful reminder and will help you to stay focused on your purpose.

LET US PRAY

Dear God,

I confess that sometimes I feel as if I do not have a life that will leave a legacy that brings glory to You. My heart breaks when I think of the painful places that have made me feel so broken inside. I stand on Your promise that You will make something beautiful out of my brokenness, and I ask You now to help me live out the rest of my days to bring glory to You, even if it means sacrificing the things I want for Your will to be accomplished in my life. Amen.

When your faith is tested, your endurance has a chance to grow. So let it grow, for when your endurance is fully developed, you will be perfect and complete, needing nothing.

JAMES 1:3-4

His Love Letter to You

My Beloved Daughter,

I know life can seem unbearable.

I feel everything you feel, and My heart breaks as yours does when I see the broken hearts and the bad things that people I created do to one another. As I told you in My Word, "There will be suffering in this world, but I have overcome this world." You will need to look up and live driven by eternity to find the power to persevere through trials and the peace only I can give. I want you to take joy in knowing that every choice you make to surrender your wants and desires for My will to be accomplished will forever be celebrated and seen by all!

Love,
Your heavenly Daddy who will soon wipe away every tear

If you are suffering in a manner that pleases God,
keep on doing what is right, and trust your lives to
the God who created you, for he will never fail you.

1 PETER 4:19

TREASURE OF TRUTH

WHEN YOU'RE TOO WEAK TO RUN,
HE WILL CARRY YOU TO THE FINISH LINE OF YOUR FAITH.

Love Questions for Your Small Group

1. At the end of your life, what do you want to be remembered for?
2. What are some changes you may need to make in order to leave that legacy?

Love Question Online with Sheri Rose

If I have no will or fight left inside me, how can
I leave a legacy?

Snap the code with your smartphone or visit the link for Sheri Rose's insights.

www.tyndal.es/YourHeartsDesire3

FOR MORE TEACHING VIDEOS FROM SHERI ROSE,
GO TO WWW.BIBLELIFECOACHING.COM.

4

DESIRING GOD'S DESIGN THAT ME AND MY MAN BECOME ONE

Fighting to Find a Heart Connection in Our Dramatic Differences

~~~

As iron sharpens iron, so one person sharpens another.

PROVERBS 27:17, NIV

WHEN I MET my husband, Steve, I was sure we were a match made in heaven. In fact, we have had the privilege of being in ministry together for most of our marriage. I wish I could tell you it's been an effortless, wonderful life for the two of us, but I would be lying to you. As I look back, I believe that Proverbs 27:17 (see above), which Steve and I chose for our wedding invitations, was most appropriate.

Our different upbringings were evident to all the guests at our wedding, which was held in the chapel at Biola University. Steve was pleased that our simple wedding cost only $800. Of course, he hadn't factored in the contribution my dad had made to the ceremony. As a popular Hollywood disc jockey,

Dad wanted our wedding ceremony to be picture-perfect . . . so he willingly shelled out an additional $10,000 for fifteen studio lights and four cameramen, one of whom stood behind the pastor the entire time so he could get tight shots of Steve and me saying our vows.

By the time I walked up the aisle, Steve was sweating profusely, not because he was nervous, but because he was standing directly beneath those bright, heat-generating lamps. They were no problem for me, since in between segments of the ceremony, a makeup artist came up to powder my nose and face. Our wedding could have come straight out of a soap opera, which was only appropriate since producers from both *Days of Our Lives* and *The Young and the Restless* attended.

Of course, I quickly learned that staging even the most elaborate wedding ceremony is easy compared to maintaining a ministry and a marriage. There have been countless days when I have felt like giving up on our marriage and our ministry because it takes so much work to understand the differences between a man and a woman. That includes how we handle our dissimilarities.

For instance, I learned to fight loud and strong by watching my parents. My brother and I would hide together in my bedroom as our parents tore into each other during arguments, often screaming and throwing things. As my dad stood red-faced with veins popping out of his neck and his hairpiece trembling atop his head, he would scream, "I want instant happiness in this home, and I demand it now!" My poor mom always screamed right back at him, tears streaming down her face. Their fights sometimes lasted for hours, usually until my mom fled our home, slamming the door behind her.

Steve was raised in quieter surroundings. His parents dealt with conflict quite differently from mine. There was no rage. No yelling. No broken furniture. His parents rarely fought—and never in front of their children. But his family also had no system to resolve conflict. That meant issues went unresolved—though not unnoticed.

Obviously Steve's and my fighting techniques were drastically different. However, neither of us had been equipped to deal appropriately with marital conflict. That led to major challenges early in our marriage whenever we attempted to resolve a disagreement. To make things even more difficult, when I married Steve I was a new Christian and had not yet learned how to channel my anger properly.

At the time, we were business partners, producing weeklong talent showcases to help models, actors, and singers connect with Hollywood agents and producers, much like *American Idol* today. We were also new parents. The strain of constant travel and some unexpected business reversals led to conflict. I tried everything to get him to react, from the silent treatment to screaming and crying. I didn't mean to play games; I just wanted to get his attention. However it didn't work. I became more bitter and he became more distant; then I assumed he didn't care about me or our marriage.

One day I couldn't take Steve's calm, cool responses

anymore. From my perspective, he obviously needed some lessons on how to fight for our marriage. I'd had enough of his "let's work it out peacefully by ignoring our problems" act. In my mind, he was being polite only to annoy me.

"Why don't you ever show some emotion and prove to me you care about our marriage?" I yelled.

Steve stood there quietly, shaking his head and looking down at the ground. Then suddenly, he turned toward the mirror on our bedroom closet door and kicked it as hard as he could, smashing it to bits.

Wow, I thought, *what a performance. He sure learns fast.*

Suddenly I began to laugh hysterically through my tears. I was so shocked I wasn't sure if I was relieved or ready to run from what I saw. His toenail was jutting out at a bizarre angle as he asked me, "Is that enough emotion for you? If it would help, I could probably throw myself on the floor and work up a good cry." We both began to laugh together as we attempted to pick up the glass fragments scattered all over our bedroom floor. In that moment I realized how much we had shattered each other just because we were different and had not been trained on how to resolve conflict. Our marriage was not the problem; it was our hearts. Neither of us had a teachable spirit.

It took several years, a lot of tears, and one expensive closet door mirror to repair the damage inflicted during those early years. I finally appreciate how differently we are wired and know it is God's design that we were raised in homes that gave us a broad perspective on people and on each other. Of course, we still have conflict, as all couples do, but we have become very good at confronting issues and moving past them quickly and effectively. We no longer scream at each other or pretend that problems do not exist. Instead we work together to resolve our differences. We also understand that we are on the same team and that it's okay not to agree on everything.

After twenty-five years of marriage, we've decided it's worth letting go of the little things and fighting to understand one another instead of allowing our differences to divide us. Think about what makes your heart melt when you watch a great love story. It's not the hero's physical strength or his beloved's beauty, is it? No, you and I are drawn to the power of true love and its inexplicable ability to prevail over tragedy and adversity. The greater the conflict, the stronger the love must be in order to resolve the issue. When the hero does whatever it takes to save the relationship, our hearts soar with renewed hope. Likewise, as we seek to truly listen and understand our men when differences between us create friction, we set ourselves up for more satisfying and loving relationships.

The Author of love and life and the Designer of our differences knew there would be conflict between men and women. The real problem comes, though, when we get accustomed to seeing relational problems solved in the time it takes to eat a bag of popcorn. Our hero and his beauty have less than two hours to defeat the dragons and overcome unspeakable challenges.

You and I are not going to magically resolve deep relationship conflicts in our own wisdom and definitely not in less than two hours. Yet I believe God's Word offers many truths to help us navigate our differences in a loving spirit.

LOVE COACHING

God purposely created men to be more rational and practical and women to be more relational and emotional. Because many times we don't understand that this is God's divine design, we find ourselves in unnecessary relational battles. Instead of fighting for the relationship, we're fighting each other. The key to unlocking our hearts is not to avoid conflict but to learn to resolve what we can, accept what we cannot, and pray for the wisdom to know the difference. If we shut down or check out when conflict comes, we need to learn to fight for one another and fight to understand our differences.

Fight for the relationship . . .

Always be humble and gentle. Be patient with each other, making allowance for each other's faults because of your love.
EPHESIANS 4:2

Because of my broken family, when I first got married I was sure that every conflict between me and Steve would end our marriage. My fear caused me either to shut down and stop fighting for the relationship, or to fight unfairly. Our goal in any conflict should be to fight for the relationship and not against it. When we're fighting to get our way about something, we should always first pray and ask God if this is His will for our relationships. When we go for His will over ours, we will find peace even in the midst of conflicts that can't be resolved.

Conflict comes no matter who we marry. We may be fighting about different things with different men, but there will always be major differences between men and women. The two keys as we deal with conflict are, first, not trying to change one another but seeking to understand what creates unity and what triggers division, and second, if our men are doing something that will definitely affect our relationships, we need to deal with it honestly and in love.

We need to ask questions instead of making assumptions, which will let our husbands know we want to understand how they feel and how they see things. We should spend more time listening and less time trying to get our men to see our point of view. I once heard a pastor say that if spouses agreed on everything, only one of them would be needed. Let's not allow our differences to divide us any longer. We are on the same team and fighting the same enemy.

Today I realize I wasted a lot of years trying to get Steve to agree with me on everything. Now I am so glad we are different, because he is everything that I am not.

We would neither sharpen one another nor complete one another if we had identical backgrounds and outlooks and opinions.

❧ *Set up a dump night . . .*

We have different gifts, according to the grace given to each of us.
ROMANS 12:6, NIV

No, this is not a typo. You read that right—yes, I said dump night, not date night. At some point, we all experience something with our men that has to be addressed because it really affects our relationship and the way we feel toward them.

When we need to clear the air, we should try not to spout it out or we'll shut them down. Instead, we can ask, "Is this a good time to talk about it or could we set up a time that I could share something with you that's heavy on my heart?" Even if we feel angry, we must try hard to keep an attitude of honor. We'll have a better chance of getting our men to hear us.

Before we get alone with our men, we should go into a separate room and ask God to give us the right words and to give our men hearts to hear. We can preface our conversation by saying, "I don't know if you mean to do this . . ." or "I'm sure you're not doing this on purpose, but . . ." We need to stick to the topic we want to address and not rabbit trail. We should avoid using the word "always" or "never" to describe their actions or attitudes. If we say the same things over and over, we may lose their attention. When we are desperate for our husbands to hear us, some of us will give our man twenty different scenarios to make the same point.

Note: Most men need time to process before they actually act on what you talked with them about. We shouldn't get discouraged if we need to remind our men of the same point weeks from now. I know it's hard to believe, but most of the time if we're speaking in love, our men are listening. When we're done, it's important to thank our men for hearing our hearts and let them know how much we appreciate the time they took to listen.

When I speak at marriage conferences, I always tell the men that if they let us women have a dump night, it will turn into a "get lucky" night.

❧ *If it is possible . . .*

If it is possible, as far as it depends on you, live at peace with everyone.
ROMANS 12:18, NIV

God knows there are impossible people who will never make peace with us. Those are the people who have no desire to work through differences. They bring much distraction and destruction to relationships because their hearts are hard and their minds are closed. They are stubborn and refuse to see things from any perspective other than their own. Unfortunately, some women are married to men with this mind-set.

It's hard to have someone like that in our lives. However, it doesn't mean we have to become like them or let them paralyze us by their actions. Our heavenly Father does not want His beloved daughters to waste our valuable time investing in those who are absolutely impossible. Whether it's a spouse or someone else who refuses to live peaceably with us, we can bring that relationship to the feet of Jesus. Our love will have its greatest effect when it's directed to those who are ready to receive it.

Look at the fruit . . .

Hardworking farmers should be the first to enjoy the fruit of their labor.
2 TIMOTHY 2:6

It takes a lot of energy and effort to make relationships work. Our time and energy are very valuable, so before we engage in any type of conflict resolution, we will need to ask ourselves, *Is this really worth fighting for, or should I let it go and give it to God?* Think about, *Will it start a relational fire that gets out of control? Is his heart in a place to hear what I have to say?* Let's fight for the things that actually bring us closer together and bring glory to God.

Pray for perspective . . .

The sinful nature wants to do evil, which is just the opposite of what the Spirit wants. And the Spirit gives us desires that are the opposite of what the sinful nature desires. These two forces are constantly fighting each other.
GALATIANS 5:17

Many times we react to what we feel, not what is real, and if we are hurting we rarely react in a way that will bring resolution. We can pray for perspective so we will not lose sight of what we're fighting for. We can ask ourselves, *Am I winning my way and losing my love? Am I winning this battle and losing the war? Will I lose this relationship?*

Also keep in mind that it's okay to agree to disagree. We can continue to pray our way through any conflict that comes and ask God to give us the words that will bring healing and hope.

Take a breather . . .

Better a dry crust eaten in peace than a house filled with feasting—and conflict.
PROVERBS 17:1

If a conflict gets out of control and we feel like we're losing control of our actions or reactions, it's wise to excuse ourselves and find a quiet place where we can cry out to God and let Him comfort us. We can then pray and ask the Lord for wisdom on how to handle the conflict.

Before taking a breather, we should make sure we look at the person we're in conflict with and let him know we love him. Wecan explain that we need to take a moment to sort things out and pray so that we don't say anything we might regret.

Too many times in our frustration we say things we regret. Better that you take a short break and come back prayed up and prepared to fight for the relationship.

LET US PRAY

Dear God,

I don't want to fight to change things that are Your divine design, so I am asking You to give me a heart that embraces the differences between my man and me. Give me a deeper understanding of our differences, the passion to fight for the things in our relationship that are worth fighting for, and the wisdom to become a blessing and not a burden. I thank You that You hear this prayer and that You will give me the kind of love and understanding that will bring glory to Your name. Amen.

Make allowance for each other's faults, and forgive anyone who offends you. Remember, the Lord forgave you, so you must forgive others.

COLOSSIANS 3:13

His Love Letter to You

My Beloved Daughter,

You are divinely designed by Me, your heavenly Father. I am the One who made you to think the way you do as a woman. Your gifts and talents are a gift from Me. I did not give you these gifts to compare yourself to others or to condemn others. The beauty of a love relationship is found when you give those you love the freedom to be what I created them to be, not what you want them to be. Your purpose is not to make others be like you, but to help empower them to embrace who they are and become a reflection of My divine design of a man or a woman.

Love,
Your King and Designer

There are different kinds of spiritual gifts,
but the same Spirit is the source of them all.

1 CORINTHIANS 12:4

. . . .

TREASURE OF TRUTH

THE BEAUTY IN OUR DIFFERENCES IS
FOUND WHEN WE LEARN TO EMBRACE THEM.

Love Questions for Your Small Group

1. What is your weakness when it comes to working through conflict?
2. What are some things that you have found help you work through conflict?

Love Question Online with Sheri Rose

What should I do if I cannot resolve the conflict with my man?

Snap the code with your smartphone or visit the link for Sheri Rose's insights.
www.tyndal.es/YourHeartsDesire4

FOR MORE TEACHING VIDEOS FROM SHERI ROSE,
GO TO WWW.BIBLELIFECOACHING.COM.

5

DESIRING GOD TO GIVE ME THE POWER TO REMAIN PURE

Fighting to Find the Benefits and Blessings of Purity

Run from sexual sin! No other sin so clearly affects the body as this one does. For sexual immorality is a sin against your own body.

1 CORINTHIANS 6:18

IT IS IMPOSSIBLE for us to understand the battle between good and evil that goes on in men's minds or how hard it is for them to fight temptation when it comes to women. Even those men who desire purity are forced to fight for it because of all the women who flirt and flash their flesh to get attention. Even our beloved King David, a warrior who was strong enough to stand before a giant, could not withstand temptation when he saw Bathsheba naked in the bathtub. The interesting thing about this story is that Bathsheba was unaware she was even tempting David.

Bathsheba was in her own home, taking a bath in her own yard, but when David's eyes saw her flesh, he lost his strength and forgot who he was: a God-appointed king. Once he lost his moral compass, he lost his senses. He caved to his craving for her and then set up her husband to be killed on the battlefield so his own sin wouldn't be exposed.

David's moment of weakness had tragic consequences as the baby conceived by Bathsheba died. But even more tragic was that a piece of David's soul died that day, and the passion he once had to be a heroic man never did fully return.

Our hearts' desire is for men to know how to connect to our hearts, but we make it difficult for them when we blind them with our bodies. We know how to grab their attention, but in the process are we trading what we want most, which is a real love relationship with them? Feeling sexy is fun, but what is the cost when we force men to fight temptation? Somehow it seems the price that we pay to get attention is not worth it. And it's really out of control when a man cannot even attend church because the women are distracting him from worshiping. Is it right that we should contribute to their struggle, or should we consider covering our bodies to help them remain strong and to set an example for our sons and daughters?

When I was a new Christian, it never occurred to me to change the way I dressed or flirted; after all, I was single, so why shouldn't I dress the way I wanted and get whatever attention I wanted? I had worked hard to lose over fifty pounds and get in shape. I was finally thin for the first time.

I loved God, but even more I loved the attention I was getting by dressing sexy. It never occurred to me that I might be causing men who were trying to worship God to stumble. Then one day, about a year into my walk with God, my young singles pastor came up to me after our church service and politely asked me if I could come to church dressed more modestly. He told me I was distracting him and some of the young men in our group from focusing on God. I know it took every ounce of courage he had to confront me and help me understand how men struggle, and even though I was a bit embarrassed and slightly offended, I'm glad he took a chance and told me the truth. Little did I know at the time that God was using this man to groom me for the book I am writing to you now.

We have no idea the major internal battle that goes on inside our men when it comes to women. The truth is, sex and women hold the key to unlock a beast inside of them. Deep down inside, our men are screaming for some relief from all the overstimulation and sensual battles that war against their souls every day. Think of it this way: when we expose our bodies to men and expect them to remain pure, it is like asking a woman to live in a house made of chocolate when she is going through PMS and telling her not to eat any of the chocolate.

LOVE COACHING

Men are ultimately responsible for their decision to choose purity or immorality. You probably know as well as I do that we cannot change men; we can only influence them. So let's do what we can to bring purity back into our society.

🌿 *Use your influence for good . . .*

I discovered that a seductive woman is a trap more bitter than death. Her passion is a snare, and her soft hands are chains. Those who are pleasing to God will escape her, but sinners will be caught in her snare.

ECCLESIASTES 7:26

Look at the influence the first lady in the human race had. Her craving led Adam to follow her into disobeying God. Eve saw something that was pleasing to the eye, and she wanted it more than she wanted to obey God. She ended up taking her husband down with her, and the Fall occurred.

Today the "fall of families" is an epidemic. We are losing our moral men of faith by the masses while pornography and human trafficking are out of control. Our men are forced to look at our flesh, whether they want to or not. They don't even have to seek it on the Internet; all they have to do is walk out their doors. Is it any wonder they are struggling to remain pure?

I've even heard men say they feel that by blinding them with our bodies, we women have ripped them off from seeing us as people rather than as objects. Deep down they hate who they've become, and so do we. Something has to change, and it has to start with us. How will our sons and daughters find the strength to remain pure and experience a pure love if no one leads the way?

❧ *Look at the bigger picture . . .*

Those who live according to the sinful nature have their minds set on what that nature desires; but those who live in accordance with the Spirit have their minds set on what the Spirit desires.
ROMANS 8:5, NIV

I know in most cases women are not tearing families apart on purpose. Sometimes a woman will convince herself that a man is so unhappy in his home that she is somehow rescuing him. However, the truth is that, intentionally or not, some women do rip families apart, stealing husbands and leaving children's lives shattered. In most cases this shattering starts with an innocent flirtation. Without even realizing it, a woman may bring a man the apple that will cause him to fall away from his family and from his faith. She may tempt him to miss out on the grand finale of his life, which comes from finishing strong and leaving a legacy for his own family.

❧ *Don't flirt with married men . . .*

For the lips of an immoral woman are as sweet as honey, and her mouth is smoother than oil. But in the end she is as bitter as poison, as dangerous as a double-edged sword.
PROVERBS 5:3-4

Everyone loves attention and it is fun to flirt, but it is wrong for a married woman to grab the attention of another woman's husband or to seek a single man's interest. Doing so messes with men's minds and weakens their will to remain pure and faithful. If you really think about it, you would not want your man thinking about another woman either.

Most of the time, you and I don't even realize what we're doing when we make eye contact and smile at a married man. And if we are married ourselves, we may not see the very real harm we can do by flirting with single men. We can honor marriage by being careful about how we connect with married men. We should be careful not to make any man feel more important than our own husband.

🌿 *Dress like the royalty you are . . .*

Let the king be enthralled by your beauty.
PSALM 45:11, NIV

Dress to impress the Lord and reflect His glory.

I know it's acceptable to dress and act any way we want to today, and maybe you are angry with me for confronting women who choose to dress sexy. I love feeling beautiful and sexy, just like any other woman. But take a look around you and ask yourself, is this the society you want your children to grow up in? Is this the legacy a woman should be making on this world? Think about all the great men who have fallen because of a woman.

It isn't fair for us to expect our men to remain pure if we are using their weakness (our bodies) to grab their attention so we can feel good about ourselves. Many of us are doing more than grabbing their attention; we're taking their focus off their families for our own benefit. I don't mean to be harsh, but how many more men have to fall before we wake up?

Before we get dressed, we can ask ourselves: *Why am I wearing this outfit? Is what I am wearing going to cause a man to lust? Do I secretly desire attention, or do I want to draw attention to God?* If we feel God is showing us anything in our apparel, our actions, or our attitudes that is causing any man to stumble—whether by tempting him to give up his moral conviction or to become more consumed with us than with his own wife—we can stop and change for the sake of helping our Christian brother keep his thoughts pure.

Our need for attention is not worth making men fight to remain pure. We can be a part of the solution by going through our wardrobe and taking an honest look at what message it may be sending. Then we can remove anything that would tempt a man sexually . . . unless it is our own husbands, of course.

❧ *Purify yourself . . .*

Purify yourselves, for tomorrow the LORD will do great wonders among you.
JOSHUA 3:5

Joshua knew that there was a battle to be won and that God was getting ready to do something great to bring a breakthrough and a blessing. But the Lord issued a requirement before He did that; He asked His children to purify themselves so He would be able to do great things in their community.

Likewise, I believe He is asking us to purify ourselves today so He can do great things in our lives and our children's lives. We may not be able to change the entire world, but we can change the world around us. We can give our men some relief and a way of escape from the temptations all around them so they can be the men they long to be. It is so obvious from the moral decay of our great nation that something needs to change.

Why not let it begin with us? We can help our men and our children thirst for righteousness. We can help rebuild the moral fiber of society. It starts one woman at a time. You may not be able to influence everyone, but even if you influence just one person to seek after God's beauty, you've done what you are called to do. You can become a classy role model who reflects your heart for Christ.

🌿 *Purify your home . . .*

Don't copy the behavior and customs of this world, but let God transform you into a new person by changing the way you think. Then you will learn to know God's will for you, which is good and pleasing and perfect.
ROMANS 12:2

Our homes need to be places of refuge where our sons, brothers, and husbands can find some relief from the mental and physical battles they have to fight every time they exit our homes. It's better that we get rid of beauty magazines and get control of the television and Internet than destroy our own families with them for the sake of entertainment.

When Steve and I were raising our son, we did not have cable TV or Internet, but we did turn our garage into a game room so Jacob and his friends could hang out and connect in a pure environment. The interesting thing to me is that even though we were one of the only families that guarded our home from these influences, the boys always wanted to hang out at our house. I feel that without even knowing why, they found our home a safe place of purity.

❧ *Pray for the purity of our men . . .*

Confess your sins to each other and pray for each other so that you may be healed. The earnest prayer of a righteous person has great power and produces wonderful results.
JAMES 5:16

There is great power in a woman's prayers to fight the spiritual battle that her man faces as he feels the sensual pull that wants to take him down. This battle needs to be won in the spiritual realm.

Pray that your man will crave the things of God more than the things of the world. Ask that any trap of temptation set for him will be destroyed and that God will make a way of escape. Pray that he will find accountability in another man who desires to be a hero of the faith. Don't give up! Do what you can to bring purity back to popularity, and keep praying!

LET US PRAY

Lord,

We lift up our men before You, and we lift up ourselves. God, show us what to do to restore purity in our lives and in the society we live in. We give You our wardrobes and we give You our ways, and we ask that You would fashion us to be a reflection of You by the way we act, by the way we dress, and by the things that we say and do.

Give us whatever influence You want to give us to inspire our husbands, sons and daughters, brothers, and any other men You have placed in our lives. Forgive us for anything that we have done, said, or worn that caused any boy or man to fight with temptation. Strengthen our men that they would be able to fight off the temptations of this world and finish strong in Your mighty power. We pray this prayer by faith, believing that You hear us. In Jesus' name. Amen.

We prove ourselves by our purity, our understanding, our patience, our kindness, by the Holy Spirit within us, and by our sincere love.
2 CORINTHIANS 6:6

His Love Letter to You

Dear Beloved Daughter,

I call you My beloved daughter, and with that calling comes a responsibility to purify yourself. You can help conquer the corruption around you by making your life a true reflection of My standards. I am not asking for perfection, My beloved, but I am asking for your purity to be a priority. I am requesting that you remove anything you do or say that causes others to fall away from Me. It is your purity that will bring My promises to pass in your life. It is purity that will give you the love and life you long for!

Love,
Your King

Get out! Get out and leave your captivity, where everything you touch is unclean. Get out of there and purify yourselves, you who carry home the sacred objects of the LORD.

ISAIAH 52:11

TREASURE OF TRUTH

YOU CAN'T PURIFY A MAN, BUT YOU CAN PURIFY
YOURSELF. YOU CAN'T CHANGE A MAN,
BUT YOU CAN INFLUENCE HIM.

Love Questions for Your Small Group

1. How did God speak to you personally through this chapter?
2. What are some ways you've found to dress yourself (and your daughters) stylishly yet modestly?

Love Question Online with Sheri Rose

What if the things I read, watch, and wear don't affect how pure *I* feel?

Snap the code with your smartphone or visit the link for Sheri Rose's insights.

www.tyndal.es/YourHeartsDesire5

FOR MORE TEACHING VIDEOS FROM SHERI ROSE,
GO TO WWW.BIBLELIFECOACHING.COM.

6

DESIRING TO GIVE AND RECEIVE LOVE

Fighting Feelings of Worthlessness

*May you experience the love of Christ, though it is too great
to understand fully. Then you will be made complete with
all the fullness of life and power that comes from God.*

EPHESIANS 3:19

THERE IS A BATTLE within most women's hearts to believe they
are worthy of love. If we believe the lie that we do not deserve
love, we end up settling for second best in our relationship
with our men. Even the most loving men in the world will
not be able to break down the wall around our hearts if we're
hiding behind feelings of unworthiness.

My mom did not feel worthy of love. As a child, she'd
been severely abused, both physically and emotionally.
Even though she later became a beauty queen and a tal-
ented singer, dancer, and actress, she had never learned to
love or be loved. No matter what I did to express love to

her, she felt it was not enough. As a little girl, I would tell her, "I love you, Mommy" only to hear her snap, "No, you don't!" Her inability to let me get close to her left me feeling rejected.

I remember thinking as a little girl that I would never do that to my own children and that I would make a big deal out of any expression of love they gave me. As a mother, I have accomplished that goal of giving and receiving love from my children, but sadly I have often failed at this as a wife. I spent years in our marriage not feeling worthy of my husband's love, and that feeling built a wall between him and me. No matter what he did, all I saw were the things he did not do, which is what I voiced.

I used to think the problem was all his because he didn't express love in a language I could understand. But now that I am older, I realize that without knowing it I had expected him to break down the barrier that had been there since my childhood. Yet there was no way he could tear down the wall of hurt that he had not built. Only God can break down that wall and take me in as His beloved child. Once I understood that truth, Steve's and my relationship became a healthy one.

God tells us to love others like we love ourselves, so if we don't learn to love ourselves we will not be able to give and receive love from a man. I know it may sound strange and even a little selfish to love ourselves, yet it is almost impossible to be in a healthy relationship with a man if we won't let ourselves receive love. And it is impossible to receive love if we haven't learned to love ourselves and extend that love to others.

Can you imagine if every night when you went to tuck your children into bed they refused to let you hug them or express your love because they did not feel they deserved it? As a parent, you would embrace them every time you could to prove to them they were indeed worthy of your love. If they refused to receive it because of how they felt, it would break your heart.

I believe that is how our heavenly Father feels when we refuse to let Him love us. But there's so much more at stake when we feel unworthy of love. When we are locked up inside, we cannot become the women we want to be in our men's and children's lives. If we do not love ourselves and do not let God lavish His love on us, it will hinder us and hurt others.

There are many reasons we may fight feelings of unworthiness. Some of us had fathers who never expressed how much they loved us, and others had mothers who did not feel they deserved love and did not know how to show love so we began to see our worth through their eyes and not through God's. We may have been abused verbally, emotionally, or physically. Maybe our first love made us feel we were worthless. Some of us had all the love in the world from our families, but we felt rejected by our peers.

The list of things we women believe when it comes to love is endless. But the truth is, how we feel will never change how loved we are by the Lord. Our feelings change constantly, but

God's feelings for you and me never change. Nothing we can do or feel will separate us from the love of God. But we will feel separated from our loved ones if we do not learn how to receive His love.

The truth is, as women, we affect everyone by how we love those around us and how we love ourselves. Women are the heartbeat in their relationships, so we truly do affect our sons, our fathers, and our husbands. If this describes you, I invite you to read the compassionate love story below found in the book of Luke. I pray that as you read it, you will realize that the way this father loves his son is the way your Father in heaven loves you . . . with an unconditional and everlasting love.

To illustrate God's love for each of us, Jesus told a story about a young man who walked out on his family, taking all his inheritance and spending it on people who did not value him for anything other than his money. He learned the hard way that once he was broke he had no one to love him and nowhere to go. He found himself abandoned by his so-called "friends." He felt all alone and unworthy of anyone's love. He had no choice but to humble himself and go home to avoid being homeless. The beautiful thing about this broken young man is what he discovered as he was walking down the road toward his father's home. This moment would forever mark his heart as he experienced an extraordinary act of love from the father he had taken for granted and left.

On his journey home, the wayward son kept rehearsing the plea he would make: "Father, I am no longer worthy of being called your son" (see Luke 15:19). Amazingly, his father was not waiting to give him a piece of his mind or heap guilt on him for all that he had done wrong. No, there he stood at the end of the road with open arms, ready to celebrate not the way his son left but the way he returned.

This Bible story is not just for a prodigal son or daughter. It is intended to show you how much the Lord truly loves you. I don't know where you have been looking to find your worth, but today is a new day and beautiful things can be birthed out of broken people. God does not love you for what you can do for Him. His love is unfailing and is offered with no strings attached. He wants nothing more than for you to allow yourself to receive His love so you can give and receive love.

If you struggle with this, it's time to move forward and break free from whatever is locking you up. First, ask God to show you how to receive His love and receive love from others. Your heart will always deceive you, but God's truth will clear the way so you can see your value through heaven's eyes. I don't know where you've been or what lie you have believed, but I do know our Lord gave His life to prove your worth. And you are indeed worthy to be loved. You are truly valuable, and your loved ones need you to exemplify God's love to them.

Before getting into the love coaching for this chapter, I want to address the difference between feeling that we're unworthy of love and experiencing a toxic love relationship. Have you ever taken a big bite out of a plum you thought was ripe and winced at the sour taste? Every cell in your mouth screamed out in defense, "Spit it out before you get sick!" Our bodies were designed to warn us of potentially harmful things, like rancid fruit. In the same way, we recognize healthy, ripe fruit, as well as whether someone is led by the Spirit by how healthy the "fruit" is in his or her life. Healthy love is a natural product—or fruit— of the Spirit living inside us. "But the fruit of the Spirit is love . . ." (Galatians 5:22, NIV).

If all we have ever known is toxic love, it may be hard to believe that we are worthy of love. I want to speak now as a spiritual mom and as someone who has experienced toxic love: freedom from this kind of toxicity comes when we realize that how we feel does not change how God feels about us. Joseph's brothers showed him toxic love by selling him into slavery and telling their father he'd been killed, but nothing they did could keep God from putting Joseph in his appointed leadership position in a palace. Nothing that we feel or that has been done to you and me can keep God from loving us. The question is, will we open our hearts and let His love in?

LOVE COACHING

 Dealing with toxic love . . .

But you see the trouble and grief they cause.
You take note of it and punish them.
The helpless put their trust in you.

PSALM 10:14

Abusive men can give their women countless reasons, maybe even justifiable-sounding ones, for why they hurt them. They grew up this way. Their mothers had horrible tempers and screamed at them. Or their fathers abused their mothers, so all they knew was how to express love in toxic ways. They even lie and tell the women in their lives that they deserve abuse and are not worthy of love.

Even the most abusive man hates himself for what he is doing to his woman, but he doesn't know how to stop, especially if the woman he abuses allows him to continue. Whatever the reason, a woman cannot help the abusive man in her life until she learns how to respond to his actions. If she continues to allow him to physically and emotionally abuse and use her, then her actions and influence are endorsing what he is doing.

If you are in one of these relationships, as a spiritual mentor, I want to encourage you not to stay in this dark place but to go to a local church/counselor/good Christian friend and let them help you. As hard as this is to hear, the truth is if you are constantly being victimized by a man, then you are no longer a victim—you are a volunteer. The Lord loves you and you are His chosen child, and He does not expect you to allow yourself to be beaten up or beaten down by any man.

❧ *Let others love you . . .*

Dear friends, since God loved us that much, we surely ought to love each other. No one has ever seen God. But if we love each other, God lives in us, and his love is brought to full expression in us.
I JOHN 4:11-12

It is so important that we understand how much our loved ones are affected by our reactions to their expressions of love. No matter what our men or children say or do, they can't meet our need for love until we come to terms with the truth that we are indeed worthy of the love we crave. When we reject our men's love because we feel unworthy, they feel we are rejecting them. In other words, they can't hear our silent cries to be rescued when we push them away. When they don't rescue us, we feel even more devalued. Our hearts close up, and without even realizing it, we shut out the men we love.

❧ *Speak truth to yourself . . .*

I have loved you, my people, with an everlasting love. With unfailing love I have drawn you to myself.
JEREMIAH 31:3

Think how powerful it would be if we spoke the truth about how God feels about us at least as often as we silently said negative things about ourselves or replayed in our minds all the hurtful things others have said about us. The truth is, we are not what others say, and if the men we love spoke hurtful words to us that made us feel unworthy, we don't need to repeat them any longer. We can speak truth out loud to ourselves instead:

"I am worthy of the Lord's love because He gave His life to prove my worth."

"I am Jesus' beloved bride."

"I am His chosen one."

"I am a daughter of the King."

🌿 *Breathe in His love . . .*

For the Spirit of God has made me, and the breath of the Almighty gives me life.
JOB 33:4

You know that feeling of exhilaration that sticks with you after you've spent time with a guy you know you're falling in love with? As you part, you take a deep breath and feel waves of delight washing over you. Or you know the joy that wells up inside when your man unexpectedly says something so sweet that you feel treasured? You replay those words over and over in your mind because doing so gives you a lift.

Even if no one has ever said anything kind to you, your Prince Jesus longs for you to breathe in the tenderness and kindness He feels toward you and has expressed in the Bible. If years of rejection or loneliness have put up a wall between you and Jesus, I encourage you to read through the love letters in this book and choose the one that speaks most powerfully to your heart. Type it out and place it in a pretty frame by your bed so that you'll see it at the beginning and end of each day.

Breathe that truth in; allow it to replay through your mind. Never forget Jesus' promise that "I have loved you with an everlasting love" (Jeremiah 31:3, NIV). In fact, put down the book for a moment and allow yourself to breathe in God's love for you. As you do, whisper toward heaven, "I love You, Lord." It will take a while, but if you continue to speak of how much you love Him, you will begin thanking Him for loving you so much. You'll learn to be still and accept how much He loves you.

Sing about His love . . .

Each day the LORD pours his unfailing love upon me, and through each night I sing his songs, praying to God who gives me life.
PSALM 42:8

When I was learning to let myself receive God's love, I would actually sing love songs to Him. Though they had been written for a woman to sing to a man here on earth, I began to understand that if I would crave God's love first,

He would meet my needs. Only then would I be able to give and receive love.

Today I love worship songs that sing of God's love for us. I blare them throughout my house in the mornings so Satan will not be able to whisper lies to me any longer. Consider doing the same. Wake up in the morning singing love songs to your Lord. Write love letters to Him in a journal. Watch what happens to your heart as you begin to connect with the only One who can help you find your true worth.

🌿 *Express love . . .*

Therefore, my dear brothers and sisters, stay true to the Lord. I love you and long to see you, dear friends, for you are my joy and the crown I receive for my work.
PHILIPPIANS 4:1

Paul was always good about expressing his love and appreciation. When we begin to speak words of affirmation to others, we will begin to feel affirmed and worthy of love too.

Many times you may want to express your feelings, but you are locked up inside because you feel so unworthy. If you can't yet do it verbally, write little love notes or text special people in your life to let them know how much you love them. That may sound like a difficult assignment right now, but I promise that once you begin to put your heart into words—whether it's in writing or out loud—you will begin to see the joy of pure love between people. All the games will end, and you will begin laying a real foundation of love.

LET US PRAY . . .

Dear God,

I confess I do not feel worthy of love. It is hard for me to believe that You even love me. Help me, Lord, to look to You for my worth. Forgive me for not allowing myself to receive Your love. Forgive me for looking to others to make me feel like I have value when You are the only one who can validate me and love me the way I long to be loved. From this day forward, I choose to let You love me so I can love others. In Jesus' name. Amen.

> *I will sing to the LORD as long as I live.*
> *I will praise my God to my last breath!*
> *May all my thoughts be pleasing to him,*
> *for I rejoice in the LORD.*

PSALM 104:33-34

His Love Letter to You

My Beloved Daughter,

I love you with an unconditional, everlasting love so you can be free to love.

My precious daughter, don't allow those who have hurt you to keep you from experiencing the joy of loving others. I know giving a piece of your heart away involves risk, but I am here to heal your heart when someone hurts you. I want you to choose wisely whom you allow in your heart, and I also want you to give those you love the freedom to fail. Remember that no one else can love you as perfectly and completely as I do. Don't look for a perfect love in people, or you will always find disappointment and heartache. If you allow your soul to settle into Mine and become one with Me, you will never doubt that I am forever and always devoted to you.

Your Prince Jesus, who can't stop loving you

May you have the power to understand, as all God's people should, how wide, how long, how high, and how deep his love is.

EPHESIANS 3:18

TREASURE OF TRUTH

HOW YOU FEEL ABOUT YOURSELF WILL NEVER CHANGE GOD'S LOVE FOR YOU.

Love Questions for Your Small Group

1. If you struggle with this issue, why do you think you feel unworthy of love?

2. What are some things we can do to embrace our heavenly Father's love for us?

Love Question Online with Sheri Rose

How should I respond to a loved one who feels unworthy of my love?

Snap the code with your smartphone or visit the link for Sheri Rose's insights.
www.tyndal.es/YourHeartsDesire6

FOR MORE TEACHING VIDEOS FROM SHERI ROSE, GO TO WWW.BIBLELIFECOACHING.COM.

7

DESIRING TO EMBRACE MY NEW LIFE IN CHRIST

Fighting the Enemies of Shame, Guilt, and Regret

> *At that moment their eyes were opened,*
> *and they suddenly felt shame at their nakedness.*
> *So they sewed fig leaves together to cover themselves.*
>
> GENESIS 3:7

WHEN MY HUSBAND, Steve, and I married, I thought I was totally free from the shame of my past. Then one afternoon shame wiped out what should have been one of the most wonderful moments of my life. My husband and I were so excited about going to the doctor to confirm that, yes, we were going to have a baby. Since I have dyslexia, my husband was filling out the medical paperwork for me. He began to ask me the questions about my medical history. We were almost done with the paperwork when he read the dreaded question: "Have you had an abortion?"

I had not told my husband that prior to our marriage I'd gotten pregnant and my parents had made me get an abortion. All of a sudden, memories of the doctor's office I had walked into when I was sixteen years old flooded my mind. Back then I was afraid, I was nauseous, and something deep inside of me felt what I was about to do was not right. My parents were not Christians at the time, but I still had some sort of conviction in my soul. I remember looking up at the abortion doctor and saying, "Is this an actual baby in my tummy right now?" The doctor said with a smile, "You're doing the right thing. It's not a baby until twenty weeks. It is just a formation in your uterus that needs to be removed."

When the procedure was over I felt so much shame, and for years after that I wondered if I had taken a life. That question was not truly answered until I was twenty-eight and lying on another doctor's table. When he asked me if I wanted to hear my baby's heartbeat, I said, "How is that possible? I'm only six weeks pregnant." I had been told— wrongly!—that babies don't have heartbeats until they are at least twenty weeks old.

The doctor then put the stethoscope to my tummy, and for the very first time I heard the beat of my son's heart. I began to cry uncontrollably. . . . My husband thought I was crying tears of joy. However, the truth is that I was crying tears of pain, shame—and even terror!

I couldn't bear the thought of what had happened, and I could not handle the embarrassment of telling my husband the truth. For the first five months of my pregnancy, I was deathly sick and hooked up to IVs to control the nausea. I was sure this was part of my punishment for the abortion

I'd had earlier. Even going into the delivery I feared my baby would die, and for the first five years of Jacob's life I was sure he would be killed somehow as a punishment for what I'd done. Shame had robbed me of joy and enjoying the first years of my son's life. I wanted so desperately to tell my husband the truth and get out from under the shame I had tried to bury in my soul. At the time I was such a new Christian that I didn't know if there was any way I could get right with God for something so wrong that had happened so long ago.

One precious Easter at the little church we attended in Sisters, Oregon, I finally found forgiveness and freedom from shame. As we entered the small, sweet sanctuary, the choir was singing about the old rugged cross. Ushers were at the door handing out big rusty nails and pieces of paper. Chairs had been set in a circle around a very rugged-looking cross with a purple robe draped over it. The pastor began to talk about Easter and the Cross in a way I'd never heard before. As he spoke, I held that rusty nail so tight that I discolored my hand. And once the pastor had defined the purpose of Jesus dying on the cross, he gave us a very interesting invitation. He said, "This nail you're holding in your hand could be your key to freedom. I invite you to write on a piece of paper whatever it is you're holding on to—shame, anger, guilt. Write it out on the paper, come forward, and pick up the big hammer by the cross. Take the piece of paper and nail it to the cross and walk away free from shame."

Oh, how I wanted to run to that cross, but an inward battle went on as I sat there paralyzed by my fear of what people would think if I walked forward. And what if people read the piece of paper about my abortion? Would I have to tell my husband if I handed this over to God?

Finally I couldn't take it anymore. I wanted freedom. Once I made the decision I felt the Spirit of God whisper, "Give Me your past. Give Me your shame."

I got up and walked toward the cross. And the moment I picked up that hammer and drove the nail through my confessed sin, I felt the Lord whisper in my spirit, "This is why I had to die for you—so I could take away all your guilt and shame."

At that moment God replaced my past shame and pain with His peace. I got home and felt like it was time to share what I had hidden from my husband. I walked over to him, hugged him, looked in his eyes, and said, "I am so sorry I never told you this before, but when I was a teenager I aborted a child." Steve was compassionate and nonjudgmental as he began to realize the torment I was under during my whole pregnancy.

Once I shared this with him, I knew I had to take one more step. I needed to let my son, Jacob, who was eleven, know he had a brother or sister in heaven. That evening I talked to him in bed, and I prayed with him as I always did. This time before entering his room, I had also prayed that God would give him a heart to hear what I was about to say. I was pregnant with his baby sister, and I did not want to go through another pregnancy in fear.

Jacob cried quite a bit after I told him, and I comforted him. One good thing that came out of that honesty is that my son stayed sexually pure until he got married. I believe that was God's grace and gift to me after I had confessed my sin. I will never be proud of the choice I made to abort the baby, but I don't want to live in the past anymore.

Shame acts like a prison door over our hearts, making us feel as if we deserve to be locked up forever. It completely clouds our vision because everything we do and say comes from our shame. Shame can control us and hinder us from allowing ourselves to love.

Shame is not new. It first appeared at the fall of man and woman. Adam and Eve hid from God because of shame, and of course blame followed shame as the man blamed the woman for his actions:

> *The man replied, "It was the woman you gave me who gave me the fruit, and I ate it." Then the LORD God asked the woman, "What have you done?" "The serpent deceived me," she replied. "That's why I ate it."*
> GENESIS 3:12-13

This paralyzing emotion can seriously affect all of our relationships, especially in the way we relate to our men. I know many amazing Christian men and women who have made bad choices that planted the bitter seeds of shame in their relationships.

I understand how hard it is to break free from the chains of shame, and I realize it's even harder to be with men who have done shameful things, leaving us embarrassed and afraid of what others will think. Some moms even fear how their children will turn out because of their husbands' shameful actions. We can't be responsible for our spouses' behavior, but we can take responsibility for our own. When we are walking through life with the chains of shame weighing us down, we must confess it! Even if it's not our shame, we need to let God have it.

As hard as it is to believe, God truly can take even the shameful things we have done and somehow use them as a trophy of His amazing grace. We don't have to continue to live in shame. Yes, we live in a fallen world, and yes, we sometimes fall into the temptations of this world and do many shameful things. However, we cannot change yesterday. We can only move forward and change the future for ourselves and our loved ones. We are more than the mistakes we make, and it isn't just about what we have done; it is about what has been done for us at the Cross!

LOVE COACHING

I'm not sure what shame you're fighting, but would you consider receiving God's precious gift of grace, mercy, and forgiveness?

Perhaps you are not bound by shame but a man in your life is, whether that person is your brother, your father, your husband, or your ex-husband. If so, I pray you would ask God to give you a heart of mercy and understanding—not to excuse or enable the wrong he has done, but to be able to give him a crystal clear picture of the Cross that can free him from his shame.

❧ Confess it . . .

Finally, I confessed all my sins to you and stopped trying to hide my guilt. I said to myself, "I will confess my rebellion to the LORD." And you forgave me! All my guilt is gone.
PSALM 32:5

The first step to shed shame is to confess it to your heavenly Daddy. He loves you, and He wants you to be free.

Take a moment and ask the Lord if there is any hidden shame in your heart. And if you feel He is revealing shame to you, confess it and give it back to Him. If there is anything from your past that is hindering you from being in a healthy relationship, I encourage you to get a piece of paper and write it down. Give it to your Lord who loves you and gave His life for you so you can be free from your past.

🌿 *Trash it . . .*

It is finished! I am the Alpha and the Omega—the Beginning and the End. To all who are thirsty I will give freely from the springs of the water of life.
REVELATION 21:6

Once you have written down whatever it is the Lord has revealed to you, walk over to your trash can and say the powerful words Jesus spoke on the cross right before He took His last breath: "It is finished!" As you speak those words out loud, crumple up that piece of paper and throw it in your trash.

Never take it out again once you've confessed it and trashed it. Don't look back. Don't talk about it anymore unless it's to help keep somebody else from making the same mistake or to help someone who has had a man in her life who made her feel shame. If you are tempted to talk about it for any other reason, don't! Remember, it is finished and you are free.

🌿 *Learn from it . . .*

Commit yourselves wholeheartedly to these words of mine. Tie them to your hands and wear them on your forehead as reminders.
DEUTERONOMY 11:18

Unfortunately, much of what I'm sharing with you in this book was birthed from the mistakes I made, but fortunately our God knows how to make a message of hope out of our messes. We must not waste the mistakes we've made; drowning ourselves in guilt will not help.

Instead, we can learn from our mistakes and let them become tutors that make us wiser and serve as reminders of God's grace and forgiveness. The Lord is wonderful about the way He writes each of our stories, and it's so much better when it starts on the clean slate that comes when we confess our sin.

Embrace your new life . . .

This means that anyone who belongs to Christ has become a new person. The old life is gone; a new life has begun!
2 CORINTHIANS 5:17

I love this Scripture. It brings me such comfort to know that my life is hidden in Christ. So is yours. As hard as it is to fight the temptation to hold on to guilt, it's even harder to live with it. Let it go. You are forgiven once you confess your sins to God. Whatever it is you are holding on to right now, I invite you to step into your new life in Christ and let go of what was and embrace what's to come. It's time to live out your faith and embrace God's amazing grace.

LET US PRAY

Dear God,

I come to You now and I confess my past sin, my shame, my regret, my guilt. I ask You to forgive me and give me the grace to forgive myself. God, help me also to forgive those who have caused shame and done shameful things. Help me to give myself and those I love the same mercy that You give me every time I fail. Give me the faith to break free from the chains that weigh me down with shame, regret, guilt, and anger. I want the victorious life of wholeness, peace, and joy in You, things that only You can give. In Jesus' name. Amen.

Today I have rolled away the shame of your slavery.
JOSHUA 5:9

His Love Letter to You

Dear Beloved Daughter,

I have covered your shame so you can be free from it. I never want you to look back because I paid the ultimate price for any and all things that you have ever done. When you confess your sin to Me, I cast it in the sea of forgetfulness and remember it no more. If you refuse to receive My gift of forgiveness, then you are saying My death on the cross was not enough for you to begin a new life. Now is the time, not for condemnation, but for celebration of your new life in Me!

Love,
Your Savior who covers shame

Those who look to him are radiant; their faces are never covered with shame.

PSALM 34:5, NIV

TREASURE OF TRUTH

IT IS NOT ABOUT WHAT WE HAVE DONE BUT WHAT HAS BEEN DONE FOR US ON THE CROSS!

Love Questions for Your Small Group

1. Sheri Rose describes shame as a prison door that can keep our hearts locked up forever (see page 85). What is your definition of shame?

2. Choose one of the Scriptures in this chapter that you think speaks most powerfully to the person who struggles with shame. Why do you find it meaningful?

Love Question Online with Sheri Rose

What if someone in my life won't let me forget the shameful thing I've done?

Snap the code with your smartphone or visit the link for Sheri Rose's insights.
www.tyndal.es/YourHeartsDesire7

FOR MORE TEACHING VIDEOS FROM SHERI ROSE, GO TO WWW.BIBLELIFECOACHING.COM.

8

DESIRING TO BECOME
A WOMAN MY MAN CAN LEAD

Fighting to Let Go and Trust His Leadership

*But there is one thing I want you to know: The head of every man
is Christ, the head of woman is man, and the head of Christ is
God.*

1 CORINTHIANS 11:3

SEVERAL YEARS AGO I was attending a women's weekend retreat in Hawaii. One morning I woke up early feeling like God was prompting me to attend a workshop on how women should love their husbands by empowering them to lead. As you might imagine, out of the thirty workshops offered on everything from scrapbooking to exercise, this one was definitely the least popular. Most women are so weary from the responsibility of leading when their men seem unable or unwilling to do so that this workshop held little appeal. Only twelve of the 2,500 attendees went, and I was one of those twelve.

To be honest, I did not want to be there. I wanted to be

walking on the beach in front of the beautiful hotel, but my heart knew God wanted me there, and before long I knew I was indeed in the right place.

The speaker was passionate and wise, and I could tell she had spent much time in prayer and the Word, so I could trust what was about to come out of her mouth. As she began, she opened an umbrella and held it above her head. "As you can see, ladies, one of the corners is broken and the fabric is a little worn, but this umbrella represents our God-appointed protection and covering—our husbands."

She went on. "Yes, they are broken, they are imperfect, and they will let us down in their attempts to lead us; however, they are called by God to cover us, love us, and lead us like Christ. Although this umbrella has a broken piece, it will still keep us covered in a rainstorm. We may feel the winds swirl around us, but if we stay close to the bar in the middle and keep our heads under the covering, we will stay dry and safe."

Then she shocked us by pulling a big knife out of her tote bag and cutting each section of the umbrella.

With every slice, she loudly said words many of us women say to our men when we are angry or disappointed in them:

"You never do this!" Slice.

"You always do this!" Thrust. *Riiipppp.*

"Why don't you ever do this?" Shred.

"Why did I marry you?"

As she continued destroying the umbrella, tears were rolling down all of our cheeks. She said, "Now this is what's left of our covering after we've sliced our men with our words." She looked directly at us. "As messy and useless as this looks, it doesn't change our husbands' God-given position as our covering, and where they fall short we can trust our Lord to cover their lack of leadership."

I was so broken when I realized what I had done to my own husband that I had to excuse myself from the room. The tears would not stop coming as I realized that in my longing for better leadership I had sliced my own husband with my words and actions. By going ahead of him instead of helping him become a leader, I had undermined his role in our marriage.

I had legitimate excuses for why I picked up the ball in our marriage and ran with it instead of giving it to my husband, and in many cases I conquered and accomplished what needed to be done. However, in my efforts to lead our family, I left my husband in the dust, and he felt like dirt.

Most of our men truly do want to lead; they were born that way. Even if we can lead better, what are we accomplishing if we are crippling them from being the leaders they are called to be?

I cried and prayed outside the door of that workshop as I tried to figure out how I could reverse the damage I'd done. And then fear gripped me. What if I let go of some things, and they didn't go as well because I had given up my leadership? Then I realized I needed to trust God to cover my children and me in those places where my husband could not. It was my job to help him become the God-appointed leader I wanted, not be the leader myself.

If we're honest with ourselves, we can see the weariness on women who have to lead. Even those women who have the energy to do it become bitter at the men they married. To make it worse, our men don't feel needed. When we nag them, they fall back from their leadership position in our lives.

As I sat there, I fought my emotions. Part of me wanted to call and ask Steve for forgiveness, and the other part of me wanted him to ask me to forgive him for not being a better leader. Something had to give, and it started with me giving up my husband's leadership position. How would Steve ever be empowered to take his God-appointed position if I did not build him up by speaking life into his leadership?

I took a chance and called my husband. I asked him to forgive me for taking the position God had given him, and then I asked God to help me empower the man I married so he could become a great leader, the kind of leader he wanted to be. I'm so glad I made that call, because our marriage was cleansed that day. I felt like I came home a different woman . . . a woman ready to stay close under my husband's covering during the storms this life brings.

God created man to be the captain of the ship, and we women are the radar. This is summed up beautifully in a quote from one of my favorite movies, *My Big Fat Greek Wedding*: "The man is the head, but the woman is the neck. And she can turn the head any way she wants."

We have two challenges going on at the same time.

Men want to lead but don't feel they can lead well, and women want men to lead but don't feel they can trust their men's leadership. Neither of us seems able to find a way to get to God's will for a man and a woman. What good is a captain if no one will get on his ship? What good is a ship in the middle of a storm if it has lost its radar . . . its helpmate? We're just as needed in the middle of a storm as the captain, and a smart captain will listen to the radar. And a smart crew (a family) will let the captain keep his hands on the wheel and navigate them through the storm.

This can be hard to hear if our husbands are not good leaders and have caused much heartache and trouble. But since we are married to them, we are going to be on their ships. Wouldn't it be best to find a way to give them back the wheel so they can feel like men and lead us through this life the way God requires them to?

Sometimes we may feel as if our help is of little value to our husbands or the men we love . . . but that's not true! When a ship is headed toward an iceberg in the middle of the ocean and the captain can't see it coming, everyone will go down unless the radar alerts the captain to the danger. Just as the sound of a siren is never a pleasant sound, it is the sound that saves lives.

Life is hard and love is even harder. Being helpmates when our captains do not want to hear our voices seems meaning-less, and it's frustrating to try to follow their lead when they have no idea how to calm the storm inside our hearts when life seems out of control. This is a common scenario between men and women, but it doesn't mean we should ignore God's plan. It's obvious our way is not working.

I don't have all the answers on how to fix this because there are so many different challenges when it comes to loving our husbands and letting them lead us through this life. But one thing I do know for sure is that shutting down, burning out, or becoming bitter is not going to calm the storm or stop the ship from hitting the iceberg. If we take a hard look, not only in our own homes but in the world around us, we'll notice there is a lack of good leadership everywhere, and because of that the foundation of the family is breaking down more and more every day. Now is not the time to give up on our men or stop using our voices to help inspire them to lead us again.

LOVE COACHING

When we first meet Gideon in Judges 6:11-13, we find him hiding from his heroic calling as the rescuer of his people, the Israelites. Gideon was in a dark hole of despair when the Lord called him out to his destiny. Gideon was afraid to believe he could become a heroic leader because of his own insecurity in the face of a sea of enemies. Yet the Lord saw beyond his weakness and fear. He saw what Gideon could become when he surrendered completely to the power of heaven.

I believe Gideon's story illustrates how most men feel

about their ability to lead and rescue us. He knew God could accomplish anything. Yet Gideon could not grasp that God was orchestrating a personal victory for him. Gideon did not consider himself a warrior, let alone a leader and a victor. He was unarmed, unprepared, and alone. The safest option for Gideon clearly seemed to be to run and hide from his appointed position as leader.

That is how many of our men feel. It is not that they don't want to lead us; it is that they fear they will fail us or fall. And if they have already failed, they fear they will fail us again.

Start with little things . . .

If you are faithful in little things, you will be faithful in large ones. But if you are dishonest in little things, you won't be honest with greater responsibilities.
LUKE 16:10

If our men have been irresponsible and we are used to leading in all areas of our marital relationship, we can look for little things to give back to our husbands. Our words will have much power when we speak to them as the leaders they want to be, not the leaders we see right now.

We can ask them for their opinions or even ask them to pray for us about something. That gives us the opportunity to tell them later how their input helped guide us or how God answered their prayers.

Beginning by trusting them with such details will

empower our men and inspire them to want to lead. Even if they've done things to break our trust, let's be careful not to bring them up. We speak life to their leadership when we trust them with little things and then build from there.

🌿 *Try to complete not conquer . . .*

As the Scriptures say, "A man leaves his father and mother and is joined to his wife, and the two are united into one."
EPHESIANS 5:31

We women can conquer a lot of things, and many times we are much better or faster than our men at getting things done. However, while we're out conquering the things that God has designed our men to conquer, we can inadvertently cripple them. Admittedly, if we've been in control for a while, it can be frightening to let go. I was able to loosen my grip by asking Steve things like, "What do you think about these five bills? Which ones do you think we should pay this week?" or "Would you mind making this call for me?"

Don't get me wrong; I'm all for being our best and having some healthy competition between men and women. However, we can be careful that while we're proving we can do everything a man can do, we don't lose our men. They will love us more if we are their cheerleaders, not their coaches. And while we may not need them to get something done, unless they lead, we will not feel loved by them—and their love is something we definitely need.

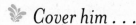 Cover him . . .

He who covers over an offense promotes love, but whoever repeats the matter separates close friends.
PROVERBS 17:9, NIV

When our husbands let us down, it's hard not to voice our anger and disappointment. We don't do it to hurt or embarrass our husbands. We are women, and we're wired to share our hearts with one another. We definitely need each other to become the women we want to be, but we need to be careful not to cripple our men by uncovering their weaknesses to everyone. Obviously we all need someone to help us sort through our feelings. I think it is best to find one or two trustworthy people who are in favor of our marriages and won't repeat our conversation to others. I have two best friends who I tell everything to because they help me see things from Steve's perspective and help me fight for my marriage by praying and sharing wisdom from the Word. I am careful, even with them, not to overshare in a way that would humiliate my husband.

Think about how we would feel if our husbands talked about our weaknesses at their workplaces. Let's commit to covering our men and not exposing them, and let's pray for them to grow as leaders.

Don't enable . . .

For husbands, this means love your wives, just as Christ loved the church. He gave up his life for her.
EPHESIANS 5:25

Because we women are so good at leading, many times we leave our men in the dust or allow them to become weak leaders. How are they ever supposed to learn to lead if we do everything for them? We are not their mothers; we are their wives. Christ asked them to love, lead, and take care of us the way He loves the church.

It's important that we not try to do things that are our husbands' responsibility unless they are absolutely necessary. Even if we can do their job better than they can, we're not helping them become the men they long to be; we are enabling them. They will see us as their mothers and not their wives, which will make us bitter toward them and produce the fruit of self-hate in their lives.

❧ *Do what you can to empower him . . .*

Sarah obeyed her husband, Abraham, and called him her master. You are her daughters when you do what is right without fear of what your husbands might do.
I PETER 3:6

I used to think it was strange that Sarah called her husband "master." I thought maybe she was even putting her husband before God. But today I realize she was a wise woman. She was empowering her husband to find his place as her leader. We can also help our husbands become godly leaders for us. Even if they do not rise up right away, we shouldn't give up on them. We can keep praying and empowering them. Whatever they do, big or small, let's encourage them. Let's be like Sarah and do whatever it takes to empower our men to be great.

Let Us Pray

Dear God,

I ask that You would show our men how to lovingly lead their families through this life. Please, God, give them compassion to cover us and a deep desire to lead us again. I want to believe in leadership for our men again, so please forgive me for anything I have done to take the position that You divinely designed for them. You know how hard it is for me to release my way for Your will when it comes to trusting his leadership. I need You to give me the kind of heart that wants to follow. This is a big step of faith for me, but I want to be a woman who builds up the men who long to lead, starting with the one You put in my life. In Jesus' name, amen.

Who can find a virtuous and capable wife? She is more precious than rubies. Her husband can trust her, and she will greatly enrich his life. She brings him good, not harm, all the days of her life.
PROVERBS 31:10-12

His Love Letter to You

My Beloved Daughter,

I am your Creator and the Captain of any storm you are in. I have created you to be under My umbrella of protection, and I have created man to be a representative of My covering in your life. I can and will cover you where your husband does not, but you must learn to trust Me to lead both of you. Take a chance and surrender your fears while following My lead.

Love,
Your King, your covering

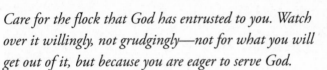

Care for the flock that God has entrusted to you. Watch over it willingly, not grudgingly—not for what you will get out of it, but because you are eager to serve God.

I PETER 5:2

TREASURE OF TRUTH

THE MAN IS THE CAPTAIN, AND THE WOMAN
IS THE RADAR. BOTH ARE NEEDED TO
NAVIGATE A FAMILY'S WAY THROUGH LIFE.

Love Questions for Your Small Group

1. Why do you think the women of this generation have become such powerful leaders in the home and the workplace?
2. What are some creative ways we can inspire our men to become great leaders again?

Love Question Online with Sheri Rose

 What if my man never steps into his leadership position?

Snap the code with your smartphone or visit the link for Sheri Rose's insights.
www.tyndal.es/YourHeartsDesire8

FOR MORE TEACHING VIDEOS FROM SHERI ROSE,
GO TO WWW.BIBLELIFECOACHING.COM.

9

DESIRING MY SON TO GROW TO BECOME A MAN OF FAITH

Fighting My Fears of Failing as His Mother

And she made this vow: "O LORD of Heaven's Armies, if you will look upon my sorrow and answer my prayer and give me a son, then I will give him back to you. He will be yours for his entire lifetime."

I SAMUEL I:II

WE ALL KNOW how important a godly, loving father is in a boy's life. You and your son are very blessed if you have a man of God in your home during these critical years. However, many mothers are battling alone to raise their beloved boys; countless others have a father in the home who has relinquished his God-appointed role in his son's life. Too many of our boys have witnessed ungodly, critical, or controlling behavior by the men in their homes rather than good, strong, loving leadership. Although a mother cannot replace the father's role in her son's life, she doesn't have to wait for the world to change its moral fiber to raise a modern-day hero who will fight for his family and remain a faithful, loving husband and father.

In chapter 1, I mentioned that I was invited to write a book for mothers of sons titled *Preparing Him for the Other Woman: A Mother's Guide to Raising Her Son to Love a Wife and Lead a Family*. To be honest, this topic intimidated me on many levels. I had my own insecurities and fears of failing as a mom, and I grew up in such a messed-up family that I couldn't see how I would ever be qualified to write a book on this subject.

As I always do before I write any book, I put this message to the test. I gathered a group of young men ages twelve to twenty and asked them if they felt they would be good husbands when they grew up. Sadly, their comments reflected their fear of women; in fact, they felt marriage was something to be avoided. Many talked as if marriage were a death sentence that caused a lifetime of pain. Others asked why they should get married since marriage usually ends in heartbreak, adultery, or divorce.

My mother's heart broke for these boys and all our sons, and their answers were enough for me to fight my fears and write that book for the sake of the next generation of marriages. As I began writing, I reflected on one of my favorite "mommy memories." It took place on a gorgeous summer evening on a California beach with Steve and our son when Jake was three. As my husband tended the campfire, Jake and I snuggled together under a blanket and watched the sun set over the sea. A young couple walked past us hand in hand, with eyes only for each other. My little boy watched them for a couple of minutes before turning his sweet face toward mine and asking, "Mommy, will you marry me when I grow up?"

I gently explained that mommies can't marry their sons. I'll never forget the ache I felt as I saw tears well up in his big blue eyes and roll slowly down his cheeks. In that moment it hit me: not only was I raising a son, I was raising someone's future husband. I decided that day to dedicate my time with Jake to helping him become a good husband when he grew up. I knew I needed to stop focusing on my fears that I would fail him and begin to focus on the fact that God appointed me as the first lady in his life, his mother. Later that night I got down on my knees and prayerfully committed my son's life to God once again. I felt a new sense of peace about being a mom as I realized that Jake ultimately belonged to the Lord and that my faithful God would cover my son where I could not.

Years later, just a few weeks before my son would marry his beautiful Southern bride, Amanda, I found myself in a reflective mood. On the one hand, I felt as if I'd done everything I could to encourage him to keep following Christ and to prepare him to be a good husband. I knew I needed to officially release Jake to his new life with his bride-to-be. On the other hand, I wondered, *Have I done enough?* I feared the years my husband and I struggled in our own marriage might affect his marriage. In my inward battle to believe I had done a good job raising him, God gave me the desire to write Jacob a very personal letter the week before his wedding. With his permission and in my hope to bring some relief to your momma's heart, I want to share it with you now:

To my son, Jake,

This morning as tears fill my eyes, I reflect on the past twenty years of life with you, from Winnie the Pooh, goody plates, and snuggles to late-night talks when you were a teen. I remember when I first heard your heartbeat in the doctor's office and the doctor saying, "You are going to have a son." Joy and fear flooded my heart at that moment.

What kind of mom would I be, coming from a broken home with no foundation? And could I take on the task of raising a son in this perverse world?

I was so afraid of failing you, and I became desperate for God, which kept me in a constant state of prayer for you, knowing that our God would cover you where I could not and cover me where I failed. What I did not know is that I was not just raising a son; I was raising a warrior and a world changer!

Today I look at your fearful heart for your future and I see a man who seeks God's face with humility,

(continued)

knowing your God is faithful. I see a man who is passionate to do something great for God's Kingdom. I see a hope in your heart that screams, "I will not settle for less than God has for me!"

Jacob, in all my imperfections and insecurities, I am honored God chose me to raise a mighty warrior like you. I know you don't know how your story will be written, and it seems unclear how you will fulfill your calling. Remember, you are not the author of your own life; therefore rest in Him. . . . He is writing your life right now. Any and everything you are about to walk through, good or hard, will prepare you for His ultimate plan.

So as I wipe the tears from my eyes and say good-bye as "Mommy," once responsible for your care, I now give you away to care for your bride. And say hello as a friend. I will always hold the memories of my little son as a hidden treasure in my heart. I pray that all you have seen and heard these past twenty years, "good and bad," will become building blocks, as you will now lay the foundation of faith and life for your new family. Jacob, you will fight the good fight, you will finish your race, and your faith will be passed down to many generations long after you're gone.

I love you, Son.

Mom

This letter was sobering for me to write because I realized that, even as I prepared Jacob for adulthood, I had forgotten to prepare myself for the day I would let him go to share his life with the woman I had raised him for. I love my daughter-in-law, and I believe it is because I have been praying for her and preparing my son to be her husband from the time he was a little boy . . . but that did not make the process of letting go any easier. He has been married over three years now and they gave us our first grandbaby girl. We are blessed that Jake has chosen my husband, Steve, and me as friends in his adult life.

It's never too late for a woman to use her influence in her child's life, and if you're a mom of a son you can probably relate to the tears I shed when I wrote this letter. No matter where you may be with your own son, whether there is a father active in his life or not, and even if your son is grown, I encourage you to keep praying, keep believing, and keep building him up. God's intervention, combined with your prayers and influence in your son's life, will help you empower and equip the next generation of men and marriage.

Just look at all the great men in our nation who attribute their success in life to their mother's love, influence, and prayers! The time to prepare our beloved boys is now. By using the weapons available to us—our undying love for them, our available time with them, our incomparable influence over them, and our powerful prayers for them—we can train them to become tender warriors. God entrusts our beloved sons to us for only a certain number of days. What a great opportunity to invest in their futures by preparing them to love and lead the hearts of their future wives!

LOVE COACHING

 Don't focus on the giants . . .

You come to me with sword, spear, and javelin, but I come to you in the name of the LORD of Heaven's Armies.

I SAMUEL 17:45

As moms we need to pray and prepare our boys for battle, asking God to help them see the giants with David's perspective. In 1 Samuel 17, I love David's confident words to Goliath: "You come to me with sword, spear, and javelin, but I come to you in the name of the LORD of Heaven's Armies." David was just a boy with no armor, but he had great faith and courage to fight what threatened the land he lived in. Because David kept his eyes on God, he didn't see the giant as too big to hit . . . he saw him as too big to miss!

I am sure the men suited up in warriors' armor had trouble believing that little David could make a difference, let alone defeat the giant. Little did they know that David was about to make history and that this battle would launch his ministry. That giant laughed at David's courage, but that did not stop David from throwing the stone that would put an end to this battle once and for all.

Today many of our sons are forced to face giants without strong male role models to teach them how to fight. We can raise modern-day Davids if we don't allow the giants to stop us from believing our sons can become heroes of the faith. Our God created our men and boys to fight the good fight, and deep inside the heart of every one of them is a David who desires to defeat giants and leave a heroic legacy.

No matter where you find yourself as a mother, I pray you will grab hold of this truth: our God is the same today as He was when He raised up mighty men in a fallen world thousands of years ago. He is bigger than any statistic, any attack, or any circumstance you are in. He is the lover of your soul, your provider, and ultimately your son's Father.

Instill a sense of honor in him . . .

I will honor those who honor me.
1 SAMUEL 2:30

You can greatly impact the success rate of the next genera-tion of marriage . . . one boy at a time . . . starting with your son. By teaching him to honor and support you and his siblings, you are training him to be a warrior who will one day be ready to fight for his own wife and children.

Help him tune in to you . . .

Share each other's burdens, and in this way obey the law of Christ.
GALATIANS 6:2

Heroes help make others' lives better. So before your son leaves the house to hang out with his friends, teach him to ask you, "How can I help you, Mom?" He will then be more likely to check in with his family when he grows up as well.

Remember you are raising a future husband and a future father, and the way he attends to you will be exactly how he tunes in to his own wife. If you allow him to tune in only to his own wants, he will not know how to tune in to others.

🌿 *Let him sacrifice . . .*

Don't forget to do good and to share with those in need. These are the sacrifices that please God.
HEBREWS 13:16

How many men today put their family at the bottom of their list of priorities? Yet Jesus asks our men to lay down their lives for us as He did for the church. Real heroes sacrifice their wants to meet the needs of others. So don't be afraid to ask your son to give up something he wants to do once in a while just to help his family. Teach your son now that a real man puts his family's comfort and well-being before his own.

🌿 *Have him read the Word to you . . .*

Make me walk along the path of your commands, for that is where my happiness is found. Give me an eagerness for your laws rather than a love for money! Turn my eyes from worthless things, and give me life through your word.
PSALM 119:35-37

The Word of God will become your son's sword, and the truth hidden in his heart is what he will use to kill the giants of temptation. Let him teach you what he has learned from reading the Bible. It will make it become real to him, and his faith will increase. Set a time at night or in the morning—whatever best fits your schedule.

❧ *Ask him to pray . . .*

Pray in the Spirit at all times and on every occasion. Stay alert and be persistent in your prayers for all believers everywhere.
EPHESIANS 6:18

Encourage your son to become a man of prayer. Start by asking him to pray for you each morning. At meals, let him be the one to pray for the food, and when there is a need, let him be the one to go before God and ask for it. If you will do this, you will make it effortless for him to step into his leadership position and provide a covering for his future wife and family. When you ask him to pray, even if it's awkward at first, you will build his confidence in who he is in Christ and teach him the power of prayer.

❧ *Teach him to become responsible . . .*

Our people have to learn to be diligent in their work so that all necessities are met (especially among the needy) and they don't end up with nothing to show for their lives.
TITUS 3:14, THE MESSAGE

You will help your son become financially responsible by letting him pay for his own cell phone or buy some of his own clothes. When he is a teenager, you can teach him to plan budgets and write the checks to pay the bills. You can also get him involved when you file your taxes.

Think about the pressure that is put on a woman whose man has not been trained how to lead in the area of financial responsibility. Help bless your future daughter-in-law by preparing him now to handle money wisely.

❧ Build him up . . .

You have been taught the holy Scriptures from childhood, and they have given you the wisdom to receive the salvation that comes by trusting in Christ Jesus.
2 TIMOTHY 3:15

Be careful how you speak to your son when he lets you down—you can inflict damage by criticizing him harshly. When he disappoints you, remind him he is made from more than the mistakes he makes. Also build him up with the truth that he serves a great God and is called to be set apart for an amazing purpose. Moms can become great encouragers who cheer their sons to their destinies.

❧ Help him keep his promises . . .

Who may worship in your sanctuary, LORD? Who may enter your presence on your holy hill? Those who lead blameless lives and . . . keep their promises even when it hurts.
PSALM 15:1-2, 4

Teach your son that the only acceptable reason for breaking a promise is an emergency or illness. If he wants to try a new sport, make sure he is committed to giving it his all—because you will not allow him to quit, even if he ends up not liking the sport or the coach.

By starting this policy at a young age, you will teach him how important it is to think through decisions and weigh consequences before making a commitment. You are teaching him, in essence, how important it is to keep his commitments. Think about all the damage done today by broken promises. Let's raise up a man of his word.

LET US PRAY

Dear God,

Help me remember that I am raising someone's future husband. I am with him for such a short time. Please give me the wisdom I need to prepare him to love his wife the way You intended. Give my son a heart of understanding, Lord. Help him grow strong in his faith and tender in his heart. Protect him from the moral decay in this world. Plant in him the desire to seek guidance from You and to grow into a godly man. In Jesus' name I pray, amen.

Direct your children onto the right path, and when they are older, they will not leave it.
PROVERBS 22:6

His Love Letter to You

My Beloved Daughter,

I know you want the best for your son and so do I.

Do not be afraid, My daughter. I don't want you to allow fear for your son's future to control the way you raise him and react to him. When you feel you cannot control what is all around him, stop and call to Me and I will give you the peace and the wisdom you need to accomplish your mission as his mother. I want you to rest in Me, knowing I will cover your boy where you cannot, because ultimately he is Mine.

I know that you love him, but I am the Author of his life and he is My chosen child. Do not fear for his future. Rest in the knowledge that everything that happens to him, both good and bad, is not bigger or better than My will for his life.

Just as Abraham laid down his only son, Isaac, I am asking you to lay down your beloved boy at My altar and rest in Me.

Love,
Your Father in heaven in whom you can trust

*Now, my son, may the LORD be with you and give you success.
. . . And may the LORD give you wisdom and understanding,
that you may obey the Law of the LORD your God. . . . For
you will be successful if you carefully obey the decrees and
regulations that the LORD gave to Israel through Moses. Be
strong and courageous; do not be afraid or lose heart!*

1 CHRONICLES 22:11-13

TREASURE OF TRUTH

THE BRAVEST BATTLES ARE NOT FOUGHT ON THE MAPS OF
THIS WORLD; THEY ARE FOUGHT BY THE MOTHERS OF MEN.

Love Questions for Your Small Group

1. Do you ever struggle with fears that you might fail as a mother or a mother figure to the kids in your life? What do you think is at the root of your anxiety?

2. What would you like to see the body of Christ do to provide godly role models for fatherless boys and girls?

Love Question Online with Sheri Rose

What if my son is grown and I feel like I have failed as a mom?

Snap the code with your smartphone or visit the link for Sheri Rose's insights.

www.tyndal.es/YourHeartsDesire9

FOR MORE TEACHING VIDEOS FROM SHERI ROSE,
GO TO WWW.BIBLELIFECOACHING.COM.

10

DESIRING A MIRACLE TO BUILD A NEW FOUNDATION OF LOVE

Fighting to Find a Renewed Passion, Purpose, and Plan

⟿

You know very well what trouble we are in.
Jerusalem lies in ruins, and its gates have been destroyed by fire.
Let us rebuild the wall of Jerusalem.

NEHEMIAH 2:17

I HAVE SPENT YEARS ministering to those whose hearts have been broken by a loved one. The truth is, many women are so burnt out in their marriages that they are forced to fight an internal battle every day just to keep going. Men have the power to lift or crush our spirits like no one else can. With this power comes great responsibility—husbands must care for their wives and live with them in an understanding way, as Christ would (see 1 Peter 3:7). But even the most dedicated of men have trouble understanding the incredible power they have to make or break us!

Often as women, we try to hide our true emotions. We

feel guilty for being hurt by or angry with the men we love. But the truth is that we just cannot help being affected by them. Like radar, each of our spirits is sensitive to our man's words—spoken and unspoken; to his motives—good and bad; to his spirit—proud or humble; and to his attitudes toward us—hidden or open.

The enemy of our souls is good at creating illusions of hopelessness. As hard as it can be to believe there is hope, it is harder to remain hopeless. Even if our men have given us every reason to give up on our relationships with them, we must not give up our God-appointed position of influence in their lives. We can look up and begin to believe our God can restore mighty men in a fallen world just as He did through the national phenomenon that continues to take place through the Promise Keepers men's ministry. With God in the picture, all it took was one broken, imperfect man named Coach Bill McCartney to motivate millions of men to do something far greater than building their businesses and their bank accounts, or creating lives filled with selfish pleasure. He challenged these men to build their character, build their faith, and rebuild their marriages by loving their wives and laying a stronger foundation for their families and future generations. Women all over the nation stood in awe as they witnessed multitudes of men gathering together in stadiums across America to learn how to take their heroic position and help restore America's families—starting with their own.

I am sure this one man never imagined how many

millions of men would actually join him on his journey to rebuild the foundation of faith and family. One thing I know for sure is our God will not waste women's tears when they cry out to heaven. He loves when His beloved daughters believe in Him, and His heart breaks for His girls when the men He created to lead and love them don't take their God-appointed position. Just because you don't see a hero in front of you doesn't mean there is not one ready to rise up.

I know this is hard to hear if you have lost the one you longed to spend your life with or your man seems to have lost his will to fight for you. Many of us women are so rightfully worn out and bitter we can't even find the strength to believe anything but bad things about men.

To be honest, I hear so many stories of heroic men of God who have walked off the battlefield and left their families to live for themselves and their own pleasure that I had to fight my own discouragement in order to write this book. I have met amazing women of faith who made every effort to faithfully help their men become great. They prayed, they persevered in love, they poured their lives into their men— and today they feel abandoned, rejected, and ready to give up their God-given role as women. But shutting down or giving up will not heal or help anything that is going on between men and women. Our God is greater than the poor choices our men make.

I've witnessed even the strongest of marriages crumble as godly couples who truly wanted their families to work find themselves in "survival mode." The foundation of love they once knew is gone, and what remains is bitterness. They are too broken to attempt to rebuild anything.

I can confidently say that Promise Keepers was birthed out of the pain, prayers, and perseverance of wives, mothers, and women all over the world who cried out to God for their husbands, their fathers, and their sons with persistence. Promise Keepers was God's answer to His beloved daughters' prayers.

Ironically, Lyndi McCartney says she was emotionally bruised and neglected for more than thirty years while her husband, Bill McCartney, was sold out to coaching football. For ten months out of the year, he worked sixteen-hour days, six or seven days a week. Even after he founded Promise Keepers, Bill did not clearly see how much hurt he had caused his own wife.

Lyndi was so depressed that she lost more than eighty pounds over seven months. Bill spoke at ten stadium events for men before he realized the crisis his wife faced. After Christian counseling, Bill finally looked at his wife's despair and emotional pain and decided to face the evidence. His conclusion was simple and profound. "I had caused this," he wrote. His wife's depression was the fallout from Bill's chronic insensitivity and neglect toward her. Her emotional defenses had been demolished through years of wanting, of waiting.

Sadly, according to Lyndi, despite all the warnings she had given Bill, it wasn't until she broke down completely that he finally began to notice her heartbreak. "Before that, he was the same as a plumber," Lyndi recalled. "A plumber never fixes anything at home. He's always out fixing everybody else's problem."

Even then, Bill felt at a loss about what to do. His heart was finally pierced by a powerful statement he heard from a preacher: "Do you *really* want to know about a man's character? Then look into the face of his wife. Whatever he has invested in or withheld from her will be reflected in her countenance."

When Bill looked squarely at his wife's face, his heart sank. "What I saw stunned me. Her face was sad and empty. Her eyes, once so bright and effervescent, had lost their sparkle. I saw pain . . . slow decay . . . emotional torment . . . she appeared drained, depleted, and unfulfilled. What had I done?"

You, too, may find God's promise that His plans are good hard to believe if you are in or have experienced the bitter taste of a love relationship gone sour. In the moment, you feel you may never truly love again.

If you are overwhelmed by the ruins of relationships around you, I invite you to read the amazing "God story" about a broken man named Nehemiah who had to decide whether to give up or look up.

In Nehemiah 2:17 we read about a city that has been shattered: "Jerusalem lies in ruins, and its gates have been destroyed by fire." The walls that once protected God's people had been destroyed and all that was left were brokenhearted people and one broken man of faith who saw the ruins of Jerusalem and cried out to God. I can imagine Nehemiah questioning why God did not stop this destruction from happening. Surely if God cared, He would have protected His own holy city. Today, many of us hold the ruins of our own lives, broken by the destructive behavior and neglect of others, and we ask God the same question. We are just like Nehemiah, living in a land of hopelessness when it comes to love and marriage.

We see the moral decay and devastation of shattered lives and the ruins of families from relational wreckage. There are many reasons we are in this mess and we could continue to blame one another, but what good would it do? The truth is, none of us ventured into marriage to see it end in misery or divorce. It would be wise for us to look at our own wreckage the same way that Nehemiah did his. What I mean is, let's do something about it. We need a Nehemiah revival today if anything is ever going to change.

Nehemiah could have given up on God and his people and finished out the rest of his life depressed, bitter, and hopeless. Instead, he chose to fight the temptation to quit, to speak life into a dead situation, and to start building. Nehemiah took a step of faith and told his fellow Israelites, "Don't be afraid of the enemy! Remember the Lord, who is great and glorious, and fight for your brothers, your sons, your daughters, your wives, and your homes!" (Nehemiah 4:14). Nehemiah refreshed the people with a new perspective on the devastation around them.

Nehemiah did not deny that there was a problem; he didn't ignore the fact that God's people were discouraged and depressed. He himself was broken by what he saw. However, he took his brokenness and did something about it. He spoke words of life, and he inspired the people to take the broken stones from the wall and lay them down one at a time to build a new and stronger wall.

With God, brokenness does not have to be the end. Pain can become the very thing that brings us into a closer relationship with God and transforms us from the inside out. Even those of us who are the most broken can speak this truth: "I choose to believe my God will not waste this pain."

Nehemiah's broken heart compelled him to faith and action. He knew that what he was asking appeared to be impossible, yet he dared to believe God. His heavenly Father was then pleased to bless him with great favor. God used Nehemiah's compassion to rebuild what was broken as He gave Nehemiah the strength needed to help his people live for a greater purpose than their own personal loss. He showed them how to begin rebuilding a foundation with a thankful heart and renewed faith.

Nehemiah's story encourages us even today with the truth that with God all things are possible. When we pray, we don't always get what we want, but when we invite God into our circumstances by faith, He begins to move on our behalf. That requires sacrifice—we must lay down our heart's desire for our Father's will—but I can't think of anyone more trustworthy than our heavenly Father.

We have all been hurt, and our hearts need healing at some level. We each hold a stone that represents our reaction to those who have broken our hearts, and we all have a choice with what we will do with the stone we're holding. We can throw it, use it to rebuild what is broken, or lay it down at the Lord's feet and let Him deal with those who have caused us pain. We may feel justified throwing a stone at those who have hurt us, and we might even experience momentary relief if they feel the same pain that they caused us. However, before we take revenge and throw that stone, we need to ask ourselves a bigger question: If we choose to throw it, who else might we hit? Our children? Ourselves? Will it help repair the damage or add to what's already done?

LOVE COACHING

The first stone will be the hardest to lay down, but it will become the stone that builds a new foundation for us and our loved ones. We may know we cannot save our relationship in our own strength; if so, we can give what is impossible to God. If there is anything worth saving in our relationship, we can ask our heroic Savior to resurrect our love and roll the stone off our hearts and our men's hearts so we can finish out this life together.

❧ *Build by looking up . . .*

I look up to the mountains—does my help come from there? My help comes
from the LORD, who made heaven and earth!
PSALM 121:1-2

Something will change inside of us and healing will begin
when we stop looking outward and start looking upward.
God can open our eyes so we can see a much bigger picture
than our own lives, and in His strength we can begin building for a greater cause.

Nehemiah looked outward just long enough to get
a clear picture of the problem but then, in his brokenness, he looked upward and sought the help of heaven
through prayer and fasting. God answered his prayers and
gave him the wisdom and favor to rally God's people and
inspire them to gather the stones that were left among
the rubble and start rebuilding. Nehemiah's reaction to
the ruins of Jerusalem caused mercy to come down from
heaven, and God's children were empowered by His
grace to do something greater than they could ever do
on their own.

Yes, it was hard, and, yes, they had to fight to protect
what they were rebuilding. To ward off their enemies, they
held a weapon in one hand as they laid stones with the
other (see Nehemiah 4:17). The entire community fought
discouragement, despair, and even deception to secure their
safety and freedom. So I encourage all of us to take a step
of faith and dare to believe God like Nehemiah did. Then

we will be a part of the deliverance and not the destruction of society.

The truth is we all have a choice as to how we will react to the wreckage of relationships around us. Even if it is not our own relationship with a man, we—along with our children—are still affected by the fallout from our society's tragic epidemic of divorce.

It's time to stop talking about the ruins of relationships and to start praying for the passion and wisdom to start rebuilding. When this life is over, let's be remembered as women who refused to allow bitterness, blame, and others' bad actions to stop us from laying a foundation of unconditional love for the next generation.

❧ *Build with grace and mercy . . .*

Be patient with each other, making allowance for each other's faults because of your love.
EPHESIANS 4:2

One of my favorite heroic moments involving Jesus is when He lovingly rescued the adulteress whom everyone wanted to stone to death. There she was exposed, accused, and without hope, and Jesus came to her rescue with great compassion. Her accusers had signed her death warrant, but Jesus provided her escape.

Because Jesus loved her, she did not have to finish her life as an unfaithful woman but as a forgiven child of God. That is how our Savior loves each of us. He is not a condemner; He is a redeemer. He shields us and exclaims like He did to the adulteress's accusers, "Let the one who has never sinned throw the first stone!" (John 8:7).

When we open our hurting hearts to His merciful love for us, we find supernatural compassion for those who have wronged us or wounded us. Our God knows how hard it is to rebuild when men have broken our hearts. To do so, we will need to find our passion by building for eternal purposes and future generations. We will not find strength from any man. Our strength comes from the Lord.

Let's do whatever we can to water our relationships with truth, love, grace, mercy, and words of life. Even in difficult situations involving divorce, we will find healing when we show the world what unconditional love looks like. No matter what the outcome of our relationships, I believe God will reward us with perfect peace as we choose to build for His glory.

Let Us Pray

Dear God,

Today I am stepping out in faith. No matter how hard it is to do, I am asking You to help me become a rebuilder of what has been destroyed in my relationship. I give You my hurt, my disappointment, and my frustration, and in exchange I ask You to give me a renewed heart for my relationship and the courage to persevere in love. In Jesus' name. Amen.

If another believer is overcome by some sin, you who are godly should gently and humbly help that person back onto the right path. And be careful not to fall into the same temptation yourself. Share each other's burdens, and in this way obey the law of Christ.

GALATIANS 6:1-2

His Love Letter to You

My Beloved Daughter,

My heart breaks with yours when someone hurts you. I know how hard it is for you to find the strength to rebuild a relationship when you feel worn out. Please rest assured that I will give you My strength to take this on if you will ask. I am the same God who gave Nehemiah the strength and favor to rebuild the broken walls of Jerusalem, and I will give you either the strength to lay your burden down and leave it at my feet, or I will give you the renewed passion to rebuild from the broken pieces of your heart. Don't overwhelm yourself by attempting to build every broken wall at once. Start laying one stone at a time. Rebuild with words of forgiveness, grace, and unconditional love.

Love,
Your heavenly Father, the Master Builder

Build up, build up, prepare the way,
   Remove every obstacle out of the way of My people.

ISAIAH 57:14, NASB

. . . .

TREASURE OF TRUTH

AS PAINFUL AS IT IS TO PUSH THROUGH THE PAIN, IT'S EVEN MORE PAINFUL TO WASTE IT.

Love Questions for Your Small Group

1. Is there really any benefit to blame, bitterness, and unforgiveness? If so, what is it?
2. How did God speak to you in this chapter when it comes to rebuilding?

Love Question Online with Sheri Rose

What does an act of forgiveness really look like when it's lived out?

Snap the code with your smartphone or visit the link for Sheri Rose's insights.
www.tyndal.es/YourHeartsDesire10

FOR MORE TEACHING VIDEOS FROM SHERI ROSE, GO TO WWW.BIBLELIFECOACHING.COM.

11

DESIRING EXPRESSIONS OF LOVE AND ROMANCE IN MY MARRIAGE

Fighting to Remain Faithful in My Heart

~⁓~

How lovely are your cheeks; your earrings set them afire!
How lovely is your neck, enhanced by a string of jewels.
We will make for you earrings of gold and beads of silver.

SONG OF SONGS 1:10-11

OUR HEAVENLY FATHER understands a woman's desire to feel loved and romanced by her man. He also knows the passion that burns inside a man for a woman. After all, He created that kind of love! Unfortunately, few Christian men know how to express romantic love the way God intended. Many men show more interest in and passion for their favorite sports teams or their jobs than for their own wives. And women everywhere are substituting their God-given desire for romantic love with chocolate, romantic novels, and movies—anything to fill the void in their marriages.

Sadly, many well-intentioned Christian leaders, pastors,

and marriage counselors have led men and women to believe that romance is only for the movies, not real-life marriages. This has perpetuated the lie that it is acceptable for men to emotionally vacate their marriages and stop expressing love and romance to their wives. The irony of this kind of teaching is that it seems to ignore the reality that men use romance, affection, and displays of love to get their wives to say "I do" and "I will spend my life with you." Because of this teaching, we have spent years trying to convince ourselves that we do not need our men to express their love to us once we're married. We are even made to feel guilty for craving a romantic relationship with our own husbands.

I don't want to offend anyone, but if this teaching is true I can't help wondering why so many of our marriages are empty and our children have pretty much given up the idea of marriage. How many affairs would not happen if husbands and wives were filling each other up instead of taking each other for granted? How much more would we influence the world around us to believe in marriage again if we publicly displayed our love for one another? What an amazing witness that would be!

How much stronger would our marriages be if we prayed and asked God to help us let go of past ways and learn to express romantic love in the same ways it is written about in the Song of Songs? This kind of love would instill faith in marriage for the next generation to see.

But before we get too discouraged about the lack of romance in our relationships, I want to defend the men in the church. First of all, most of them have very few role models who express outward romantic love to their wives. Second, many men who desire to be romantic are laughed at by their buddies. Third, Christian leaders are overwhelmed by the miserable marriages they are trying to help. They are doing the best they can but feel as if they have run out of answers. They have come up with some pat answers in an effort to bring relief to all the loveless and lonely marriages in the church. They've settled for phrases like, "Marriage was not made to make us happy. It was made to make us holy," or "Marriage was never intended for romance."

Whoever is teaching the church that romantic love is not God's will for marriage needs to read the following verses from the Song of Songs, which reveal some of God's deeper insights on romantic love:

> *You are beautiful, my darling, beautiful beyond words. Your eyes are like doves behind your veil. Your hair falls in waves, like a flock of goats winding down the slopes of Gilead. Your teeth are as white as sheep, recently shorn and freshly washed. Your smile is flawless, each tooth matched with its twin. Your lips are like scarlet ribbon; your mouth is inviting. Your cheeks are like rosy pomegranates behind your veil.*
>
> SONG OF SONGS 4:1-3

This is just one small section from the Song of Songs, which records an extremely expressive and romantic conversation that is taking place between a man and a woman who are married. And yes, it is recorded in the bestselling book of all time . . . the Bible. I am convinced after reading the Song of Songs that romantic expressions of love between a man and a woman do not only hold *them* together. Just as important, this Scripture speaks to a world that is watching how we love one another. Nothing brings more glory to God than when a husband and a wife love each other in the way God intended. God is definitely pleased when a man and a wife romantically express their love and appreciation for one another. The truth is, it isn't chick flicks that cause women to desire romantic love; it is our Creator, who wired us to crave the affection of our husbands! I think deep down men want to romance us as much as we crave it, but they have not been taught that this type of expression of love is actually glorifying to God.

When I got married I was sure I would never be tempted by another man; after all, it was adultery that destroyed my parents' marriage, and if I were to be completely honest, I was pretty judgmental of any Christian who fell into an affair, whether it was a physical or an emotional one.

Even though I knew Steve loved me, I didn't feel close to him because he did not know how to express romantic love the way I craved. Somehow I thought he did not love me enough to make the effort, but the truth is he had never been taught.

In defense of my husband, I was raised by a crazy father who expressed love in insane ways. For example, when he first began dating my stepmother, he wanted to lavish her with love. At the time, she was working as a waitress, so he arranged to have a local florist deliver two dozen red roses to her every hour for her entire eight-hour shift. By the eighth hour, her manager came up to her and told her that if one more rose was delivered to their building, my stepmother would lose her job. She had to call my dad to tell him that, as much as she appreciated his expression of love, she couldn't afford to lose her job.

His expressions of love didn't stop even after they were married. Because he did advertising for Marineland, he knew they had elephants. Since my stepmom loved collecting elephants, he had the park deliver an elephant to our front door, along with twenty dozen roses. All the local news stations covered the story of his love while she rode the six-thousand-pound animal in our neighborhood. But after that escapade with the elephants, we were never again invited to any of our neighbors' homes for summer barbecues.

Now that is hard for any man to compete with! At the same time, my husband would have laid down his life for me and served me in many ways I took for granted, so from his perspective he could not understand why I needed those romantic moments to feel loved. Good thing for him I have no desire to have jungle animals delivered to my door—nor do I want more roses than the square footage of my home.

But like most women, I still longed for more romance, love notes, and special date nights. Finally one night seven years into our marriage I broke down. I told Steve I needed him to fill my love tank—that I had been running on empty for a long time when it came to romance. Unfortunately, Steve did not have any idea how to fill me back up, so he did what many men do: he unintentionally ignored his bride's cry for romantic love and affection.

After a while, I grew tired of waiting for my prince to romantically rescue me, so I convinced myself I did not need that kind of love and attention. Without even realizing it, I allowed my heart to shut down completely so I could no longer feel anything for my husband. Somehow this made me feel safe because I could no longer be disappointed, but sadly I began to lose my desire to be close to Steve.

My numbness also built a wall of resentment around my heart. The sad thing about this was that my husband really loved me, but he was just as locked up to express it as I was to receive it. Needless to say, this left our marriage wide open to the enemy's trap of temptation. Eventually, temptation did knock at the door of my heart in the form of another man—a friend whom Steve and I had led to the Lord. We had even introduced him to his wife. He was like a brother to me, so my defenses were down and I did not protect my heart.

This man spoke words that unlocked the woman I wanted to be, and his kindness and encouragement began to break down the walls of my heart. He listened to me as if he really hung on to every word, and he even prayed for me when I was hurting. I began to justify that this relationship had to be a gift from God.

He had all the right words and gave me the kind of

attention I longed for in my marriage. I became addicted to his phone calls and craved time with him more than with my husband or the Lord. Everyone who saw me during this time said how happy and healthy I looked.

For three months this blissful affair of the heart continued. Somehow I convinced myself that this was God's will. After all, we were not physical, so our contact seemed innocent. *What is wrong with having a good male friend, even if he is married?* I thought.

The list of excuses I came up with was endless. Deep down I knew my heart and my marriage were headed for destruction, but I felt as if I could not stop. This affair of the heart had so much power over me that I almost gave up all I cherished—my marriage, my ministry, my family, and my legacy.

Even though we never had a physical affair, we had an emotional one—an affair of the heart. I was out of control and could not find my way back to sound judgment. Finally I confessed and cried out to God, and He broke the spell the next day when I saw this man's wife, pregnant with their first child. I was mortified when I realized I had been taking the heart, time, and attention of someone's husband and the daddy of a child. I thought back to my own parents and how affairs had destroyed my family foundation when I was young.

I was so ashamed when I realized where the relationship with this man could have gone. I pictured myself in heaven one day, facing his child who might ask me, "Why did you steal the daddy God gave me?" What would my legacy be if I used the hearts of other women's husbands to meet my own needs?

I could not believe that I had become the other woman without even realizing it. *How could this happen to me?* I thought. *I am in women's ministry, and I love helping women find their true love in Christ.* I wanted to run away from my own feelings and actions, but I had no idea where to go or how to reverse the damage I had done to this brother in the Lord by allowing him to become my addiction.

Everything came to a bitter end, and it felt like a death. How could I find my way back to my husband's heart? Then to my complete surprise, God used my husband to rescue me. When Steve discovered my hidden affair of the heart, he did not condemn me. Instead, he came to me with tears in his eyes and roses in his hands and said, "This was my fault for not expressing how much I love you in the romantic way you desired."

Steve's expression of love that day did more than rescue me. It made him my hero, and it saved our marriage. Today I am more in love with my husband than ever. His extraordinary expression of love that day put me back where I really wanted to be all along: in his arms.

Recently Steve and I drove with a group of kids in their twenties through Southern California, and I reached over to hold my husband's hand in the car. I had no idea how much that small expression of love was impacting the kids in the backseat until later that evening when they said, "When we saw you holding hands in the front seat, you and your husband restored our hope in a happy marriage." Now that sounds extreme even to me, but it also shows how desperately our children and young people need to see us express love to one another.

Today my man has learned the art of mush. We have now been married for twenty-five years, and we both joke that seven of those were the best years of our lives. We spent so many of those precious years ignoring each other's needs, pretending to be happy, or fighting the temptation just to give up on our marriage. How I wish someone would have shown us out of the Song of Songs that romantic expressions of love are part of God's plan for marriage. Then we could have enjoyed the kind of romantic love that would bring glory to God and enhance our marriage much earlier.

LOVE COACHING

Appreciate even the littlest expressions of his love . . .

Oh, how beautiful you are!
How pleasing, my love, how full of delights! . . .
I am my lover's,
and he claims me as his own.
SONG OF SONGS 7:6, 10

Sometimes we haven't been romanced in so long and we've become so weary waiting for it that when our men give us even the smallest romantic expression of love, we forget to feed that fire inside them that would motivate them to continue with the romance. Even if our husbands just bring us a cold drink or tell us we're beautiful, we need to be careful not to be sarcastic but to sincerely show appreciation. We need to avoid one-liners like "It's about time" or "What did you do with my husband? He would never do something like this."

My dad would sometimes write love notes on toilet paper and leave them for my stepmom to find. When she came out of the bathroom with one of them, she'd be as excited as if she'd won the lottery of love. She'd give him a hug, thank him for his words, and tape the toilet paper love note to the mirror.

Our feelings will follow our actions, and their actions will be determined by how we act and react to them. So we need to keep the bigger picture in the forefront and make a big deal about anything our husbands do that resembles an outward expression of their love.

❧ *Flirt with your husband . . .*

Kiss me and kiss me again,
*   for your love is sweeter than wine.*
How fragrant your cologne;
*   your name is like its spreading fragrance.*
*   No wonder all the young women love you!*
Take me with you; come, let's run!
*   The king has brought me into his bedroom.*

SONG OF SONGS 1:2-4

Yes, believe it or not the above passage—the words of a wife to her husband—is in the Bible.

I know in a perfect world our men would start the flirting and romancing, but we are called to be helpmates to our men. So let's help them express their love to us by modeling it for them. If we keep waiting for them to make the first move, we will all lose what we want. After all, isn't true love more about what we can give than what we get from the ones we love? Let's begin to build a different kind of "happily ever after" . . . the kind that begins with us. When it's all said and done, let's do what we can to instill hope in the next generation before the foundation of marriage becomes extinct.

❧ *Don't feed your desire for any other man . . .*

When you follow the desires of your sinful nature, the results are very clear: sexual immorality, impurity, lustful pleasures.
GALATIANS 5:19

We must not feed our desire for any man other than our husband. If a married man or any man who is *not* our husband is giving us too much attention, we should shut that door quickly before it is too late. I know from experience how easy it is to entangle yourself in such attention when you feel empty inside. If we're in that situation, we need to go to our husbands and be honest with them. We need to let them know we want to connect with them and not with anyone else. And we should also get someone to hold us accountable and pray for us so we don't fall. All the fun in the world will not be worth the pain if we fall into the trap of temptation.

Many people—married and single—feel attracted to married individuals. Those feelings are normal, but if we put those feelings into words, they become reality and it will be harder to escape the trap of an affair. No matter what we're feeling toward a married man, we must not put it into words. Nothing about it would bring glory to God, and it would not help that man grow closer to his wife. Let's extract ourselves as quickly as we can and protect the sanctity of marriage and our own heart.

❧ *Be honest in love . . .*

Speaking the truth in love, we will grow to become in every respect the mature body of him who is the head, that is, Christ.
EPHESIANS 4:15, NIV

One of the main reasons we move away from our spouses is because our love tanks are empty. We're so afraid our husbands won't fill them up that we're not honest with them about how we really feel.

If you are married, I want to encourage you to be honest with your man if you feel unloved. But before you speak with him, pray that God will prepare his heart to hear yours. Also remember that expressing love is generally easier for women, so do little things to fill his love tank so he will be inspired to fill yours.

I can't help but wonder how many women never let their men know how they're really feeling or show them that they need to feel treasured. My husband definitely loves me, but when we first got married he was not accustomed to expressing his romantic feelings. In defense of him, he had no idea how unloved I felt for much of our marriage.

❧ Be gentle and affirm him . . .

A gentle answer deflects anger, but harsh words make tempers flare.
PROVERBS 15:1

It's easy to get so frustrated by the things our spouses do that irritate us that we forget to look for the little things they do that we should be grateful for. Nothing will build our relationships more than looking for the best in our men and looking for little ways to affirm them. Whenever they do something to express their love for us, no matter how big or small, we should make a big deal out of it. Most men are motivated when their women show their appreciation.

Many times men are afraid to show their affection because they feel we will reject them out of our frustration and anger. Truthfully, most men do not know that when we give them the silent treatment it's a clue that we actually need to talk, so we need to affirm them any time we can instead.

LET US PRAY

Dear Lord,

Teach me to see the man You have placed in my life through Your eyes. I confess that many times my marriage does not reflect Your love. I lift up my man before You and ask that You would give him a tender heart toward me and help him make the kind of expressions of love that glorify You in our marriage. Put a Song of Songs kind of love back in our hearts and resurrect our desire to demonstrate that kind of love to one another.

I pray this prayer because it's according to Your Word. Help me to forgive and forget all the things my husband has not done and embrace the things he has done for me. I pray that my relationship will become so fulfilling that Your love will flow out of me in a way that brings glory to You. Amen.

Temptation comes from our own desires, which entice us and drag us away.
JAMES 1:14

His Love Letter to You

My Beloved Daughter,

I know how hard it is to keep a commitment when the feelings are no longer there.

I am your faithful heavenly Father, and I can renew your heart, your strength, and your mind.

Remember I have set you apart for a higher calling; therefore, I never want your commitment to someone you love to be based on how you feel, but on your faithfulness to Me.

I am with you and am always faithful. When you feel tempted, I want you to call out to Me and allow Me to make a way of escape. When you feel weak, let Me be the one to give you a fresh perspective on love and commitment. You are destined to finish strong.

Love,
Your faithful God

Place me like a seal over your heart,
*   like a seal on your arm.*
For love is as strong as death,
*   its jealousy as enduring as the grave.*
Love flashes like fire,
*   the brightest kind of flame.*

SONG OF SONGS 8:6

TREASURE OF TRUTH

ROMANTIC EXPRESSIONS OF LOVE ARE THE
PERFECT GIFT EXCHANGE BETWEEN A MAN AND WIFE.

Love Questions for Your Small Group

1. Why do you think so many Christians' marriages lack romance?
2. What actions could you take to better express love to your man and help him express love to you?

Love Question Online with Sheri Rose

 What if my husband is not the romantic type?

Snap the code with your smartphone or visit the link for Sheri Rose's insights.
www.tyndal.es/YourHeartsDesire11

FOR MORE TEACHING VIDEOS FROM SHERI ROSE,
GO TO WWW.BIBLELIFECOACHING.COM.

12

DESIRING TO BELIEVE GOD CAN CHANGE A MAN AND SAVE A MARRIAGE

Fighting to Forgive and Forget the Former Things

⌒

Forget the former things;
do not dwell on the past.
See, I am doing a new thing!

ISAIAH 43:18-19, NIV

HOW DO WE FORGET the former things? Is there some magic prayer that wipes out our memories so we won't feel the pain of our past? I wish I could say that this is the way to find a new foundation for your life. Yet God teaches us through Isaiah 43 that our past does not determine our future. He wants us to embrace the new beginning He offers us and to stop living in yesterday. However, to let go of our past, we will have to leave it where it belongs . . . at the Cross.

I was powerfully reminded of this again through Alice, whom I met recently at a retreat. I had been talking about rebuilding relationships and when I finished, I walked over to the door to say good-bye to each of the ladies. I loved hearing how God spoke to them throughout the weekend, and Alice gave me renewed hope. She was seventy years old and had been married over fifty years.

I was captivated by the joy that lit up her face. She radiated from the inside out, and her smile made me feel at home. I thought Alice must have lived a wonderful life to glow with God's glory the way she did. I had to ask her what her secret was. Her response reflected a woman who was beautifully broken.

She said, "When I lost the husband I loved to my best friend, I lost everything that was dear to me, including my children. However, I discovered how much my Lord truly loves me because of that loss, and I have never been the same because of His love."

My eyes welled with tears as she shared with me the story of how her husband had served her divorce papers on their fortieth wedding anniversary. Devastated and overwhelmed by grief, she set the papers aside without signing them. She fought to understand why God did not protect her marriage after all she sacrificed to remain faithful, even in the hard and unhappy years.

Despite their challenges, she said she loved this man and never dreamed she would be alone in her older years. Though they lived apart for seven years, something inside her soul continued to keep her from signing those divorce papers. Late one night, though, she finally decided to move on and let go of the man she loved by signing the papers. Once she had done so, she felt free for the first time in many years.

Until the doorbell rang. It was 2 a.m., and she was a little fearful of who might be at her door in the middle of the night. When she opened the door, she was shocked to see her husband, Bill, on his knees with tears in his eyes and torn-up divorce papers in his hand.

He looked into her eyes and asked her for something he did not deserve: "a chance to finish my life with you." Bill told her he had just awakened from a dream he believed God had given him, showing how his actions were crumbling the foundation of the faith of his children and grandchildren—all for the sake of his own pleasure. When he woke up, he could not wait until morning. He had to run to his wife.

He knew he owed her a sincere apology, but he wanted so much more. He wanted a second chance, and he was willing to do whatever it took to rebuild what he had broken in her heart. She stood there silently until she heard the Lord whisper to her, "Today, Alice, is the day I am giving you a choice between life and death for your family. I am asking you to trust Me with this broken man and choose life, so that your legacy of faith can live on in your children through your obedience to Me."

She asked for a few days to pray; Bill told her to take whatever time she needed to decide.

Alice said she fought through the biggest internal battle she had ever experienced as she reflected on the past seven years away from this man. After all, she had finally healed from his betrayal and feared she might reopen the wound that had taken so long to heal. She wrestled through every emotion—from feeling ripped off, being rejected, and now being offered to be rescued.

Alice knew her choice would write the rest of her life story and her husband's story. If she refused to give him another chance, none of her kids would blame her. As a matter of fact, just a few days earlier all her children had let her know they were cutting their dad off from seeing his grandchildren because of what he had done to destroy their family.

After many tears and much prayer for the strength to forgive her husband, Alice surrendered to God's will and gave up her rights to take revenge. God blessed the hard choice Alice had made to forget the former things and finish her life with her husband in spite of all he had done.

The next day, Alice and Bill called all their children and grandchildren and asked them to come to their house so they could tell them the good news of their reconciliation. However, their children did not applaud Alice's choice. Their anger toward their father blinded them from seeing the eternal blessing that was to come to them and their children. It took years for them to embrace a new beginning with their parents.

Alice felt she had lost her family the first time when her husband walked out, and then seven years later she lost her children and grandchildren when she welcomed him back into her life. However, God proved His faithfulness, because during the next two years without their children in their lives, Alice and her husband grew closer to each other than they had ever been.

Today Alice says she feels like she is married to a brand-new man who adores her and walks humbly with God. They are now in a marriage ministry together, helping other couples find a new beginning with God. Bill knows all he needs is God's grace and his wife's love.

Yet this love story gets even better. One Christmas Eve a few years after the couple reconciled, their four children and twelve grandchildren showed up at their door. They told Alice, "If you and Dad can forget the former things and build a new beginning together, then we want to join you."

"As much as I wanted to make him pay the price for all that he had done," Alice admitted, "I am so thankful I took a chance to rebuild a broken man and our broken family by using whatever years I had left with him to rebuild many marriages."

Yes, Bill was wrong, and yes, he was unfaithful and caused much damage to many lives, including his own. There is no excuse for his actions, and Alice had every right to make him suffer for what he had done. However, her extremely hard decision to forget the former things will leave a legacy of love that will live on long after they are gone.

Most men don't get married with the intention of being unfaithful to their wives. That was certainly true of Bill, who had asked Alice to marry him so he could share his life with her. But like many men, Bill lost his moral compass in a moment of weakness and paid a huge price.

When I speak of Bill and men like him, I'm not talking about immoral men who continue to live lives of unfaithfulness. I'm talking about broken men, wounded warriors who long to find the faith to believe they can get up from where they have fallen and walk by faith once again.

If you are married to a man who has fallen, asked for forgiveness, and is desperate for a fresh start with you, please ask the Lord to give you a heart to start over. Many times the most significant change happens in a man's heart when his wife willingly loves him most when he deserves it the least . . . the way the Lord loves you and me.

I am not going to say this will be easy if your man's actions have hurt you. But I will say this truth: when a broken man truly repents and turns to God, he will become a better man. It takes great courage for a man to come out of hiding, face his family, confess his sin, and cling to his wife again. If your man is wounded, has sincerely repented, and wants to rebuild his life with you, I encourage you to give him another chance. It would be a tragedy to let another woman reap the benefits of the pain you had to go through when your man hurt you.

I don't know what you have experienced, but I have dear friends who have walked through horrific circumstances with their Christian husbands. Yet today their marriages have been restored and their husbands walk humbly with their God and will do whatever it takes to make things right with their wives. You, too, can give your man a chance to become the hero he longs to be by allowing him to repair the damage he has done.

I have seen so many marriages become even stronger when a man finally realizes how much he wants and needs his wife by his side. No matter how weary we feel, our Father in heaven wants to refresh us and renew our passion for His people. He'll equip us to fight the good fight so we can finish strong. Remember, the life we live here won't last long, but the legacy we leave will last forever, and the way we face and fight our battles in this life will determine our legacy.

I know it's hard to let go of the past—in fact, we may never forget it—but we can use it for God's glory. God has entrusted me with pain, and I know He has entrusted every other woman with pain as well. No matter how it appears, He is with us in the fire, and the flames will not consume us. He is with us in the lions' den, and He will keep the lions from devouring us. He is with us in the deep waters of great trouble, and He will not let us drown. And when we take our very last breath, He will be there to carry us over the threshold from this world into a heavenly place where no one will ever hurt us again and where every tear will be wiped away once and for all. For now, let's live driven by eternity and fight the good fight, finish our race, and leave a legacy for our children's children. It can all begin with us.

LOVE COACHING

🌿 *Make divorce the last option . . .*

"The man who hates and divorces his wife," says the LORD, the God of
Israel, *"does violence to the one he should protect."*
MALACHI 2:16, NIV

God says in His Word that you and I have the right to
divorce our husbands if they have been unfaithful to us.
However, He doesn't say He *wants* us to divorce them. As
a matter of fact, His Word says He hates divorce. That
doesn't mean He hates you or your husband if you have
divorced. He is a loving Father, and He knows the devastat-
ing brokenness inside of men and women who have had
to walk through divorce. He also knows the horrible pain
people experience when their spouses are unfaithful.

I don't know where you are with your man today. If he
has cheated on you, then you have every right to give up
on him, and no one would even blame you. But if there
is any chance of saving your marriage and helping restore
your wounded warrior . . . take it! Doing so will likely be
difficult at times. Memories of all that he has done to you
will haunt you, and you will have to fight to move forward
from those painful places. But it will be worth every bit of
energy and time to save your marriage.

Yes, if your man has cheated on you or fallen into some
sort of sin that has hurt your family foundation, it is wrong,

but two wrongs won't make anything right. Something amazing will begin inside of your soul when you choose to love the one most who deserves it the least. Healing will begin!

Look at his heart . . .

We love because he first loved us.
1 JOHN 4:19, NIV

God knows you have every right to feel bitter and want to make your husband pay for what he's done if he has been unfaithful to you.

But you must ask yourself the bigger question: are you winning the battle and losing the war? The truth is that deep down what you probably want is your man back, even if you don't feel like it right now.

If he is truly broken and repentant, then look at your husband and your marriage with eternity in the forefront of your mind. It is there you will find the strength to persevere. You've come this far, so don't look back. Keep moving forward. Remember, too, that forgiveness does not mean you will not feel pain; it means you have decided not to pay him back for what he has done.

Let your children be real . . .

Give all your worries and cares to God, for he cares about you.
1 PETER 5:7

If your kids are forced to hold their sorrow and anger in, they will act it out in harmful ways. They need to express their hurts and anger. Don't fuel their anger, but acknowledge their pain and pray with them. Let them know you don't have all the answers, but that you all will make it through this time with God's strength. Reassure them that even if their father has been unfaithful or forsaken them, their God is forever faithful and will never forsake them.

❧ *Think of your husband as a brother . . .*

We are not fighting against flesh-and-blood enemies, but against evil rulers and authorities of the unseen world.
EPHESIANS 6:12

When we are fighting to forgive or forget the past, we can think about this scenario. . . .

If we had a brother who cheated on his wife and then came to us totally broken for what he had done, what would we say to him? If he asked us to help him find his way back to his wife's heart, how would we help him?

We are in a war, and we need to remember we're on the same team. We need to fight for the relationship and stop fighting against each other. When it's all said and done, those of us who are saved will spend eternity together.

❧ *Pray for God's will . . .*

Pray in the Spirit at all times and on every occasion. Stay alert and be persistent in your prayers for all believers everywhere.
EPHESIANS 6:18

When we are in a relational battle, it is hard to see clearly what is actually going on. We may get hurt and say hurtful things. The last thing we feel like doing is praying for the person who hurt us, especially if it was our husband. Those closest to us have the ability to cripple us from walking out our faith in a way that glorifies God if we're not careful and prayed up.

Yet the Bible says greater is He who is in you than he who is in the world (1 John 4:4), meaning you will need to draw from the Spirit of the living God who dwells within you. The best way to do that when your relational battles seem out of control is to pray for God's will in your relationship. This takes the feelings out of the prayer and puts your heart in a position to receive what God asks you to do. If your goal is to seek God's will rather than your rights, you will succeed.

🌿 *Don't look back . . .*

Forgetting the past and looking forward to what lies ahead, I press on to reach the end of the race and receive the heavenly prize for which God, through Christ Jesus, is calling us.
PHILIPPIANS 3:13-14

None of us will forget the former things or be able to become the new creation we were created to be if we keep talking about what was. To move forward, we'll need to focus on ways to create new conversations with our husbands. It may feel uncomfortable at first, but the more we put effort into talking about hope for the future, the easier it will become for us to let go of the past.

Let's embrace today and let our hearts look forward. Rather than thinking of the battle, we can keep our eyes fixed on what is being birthed inside of our men. And we need to remember that a setback in our marriages does not mean we're not set free. In other words, even if our husbands begin to act in their old ways, let's not panic. We can come to them in honesty and love, letting them know we're standing in the gap and praying for them. This will empower our men to continue to move forward in their walk with God and in our marriages.

LET US PRAY

Dear God,

I confess I am hurt, I am angry, and I am fighting to forgive and forget the former things. There is no way I can do this in my own strength. I need You to help me see the bigger picture. Only You, Lord, can write a new beginning from a bad ending, so I choose to trust You with this relationship and willingly lay down my wants for Your will to be accomplished in my marriage.

I need Your strength to fight for my marriage and my family. Please, God, give me eyes to see my husband the way You do—as a new creation, completely forgiven. Create in me a new heart to love him once again, and help me forget the former things so You can do a new thing in our marriage. In Jesus' name, amen.

Forgive your people who have sinned against you. Forgive all the offenses they have committed against you. Make their captors merciful to them.
1 KINGS 8:50

His Love Letter to You

My Precious Daughter,

Don't give up on love because of others' actions. Your heart ultimately belongs to Me. I will use your deep pain for a divine purpose. Many times you will find healing when you choose to love others the most when they deserve it the least, the way I love you. I too have felt great pain, rejection, and anger. But we can go through every trial together. Hand in hand, I will lead you back to My place of peace. The sun will shine on you again, and your hope will be restored once again.

Love,
Your heavenly Father who will never leave you nor forsake you

We love each other because he loved us first.

1 JOHN 4:19

. . . .

TREASURE OF TRUTH

TO FORGET THE FORMER THINGS, WE WILL HAVE TO LEAVE OUR PAST WHERE IT BELONGS . . . AT THE CROSS.

Love Questions for Your Small Group

1. What do you think about Alice's decision to return to her husband?

2. Do you know of any relationships for which our group should be praying for reconciliation? Discuss this with this group, and then spend some time praying for these relationships.

Love Question Online with Sheri Rose

 What should I do if my children refuse to forgive the man who hurt me?

Snap the code with your smartphone or visit the link for Sheri Rose's insights.
www.tyndal.es/YourHeartsDesire12

FOR MORE TEACHING VIDEOS FROM SHERI ROSE, GO TO WWW.BIBLELIFECOACHING.COM.

13

DESIRING TO GLORIFY GOD BY SHOWING HONOR AND RESPECT

*Fighting the Frustration Caused
by Dishonorable Actions and Attitudes*

~~~

*Respect everyone, and love your Christian brothers and sisters.
Fear God, and respect the king.*

1 PETER 2:17

A FEW YEARS AGO I was invited to address over five thousand men at a conference. I was asked to express the heart of a woman and to show the men how to better love and understand their wives. The topic they requested was "What Women Want."

To be honest, this particular invitation seemed very strange to me since I am in women's ministry and had been writing His Princess books.

I remember sitting at my desk and just staring at the e-mail invitation, battling to believe God would open this door for me to address five thousand men. Even harder for me to believe was that I could ever convince these men to listen to me about what women want. I fell to my knees and cried out to God, "Who am I to speak into these men's lives about loving their wives? What right do I have?" As I prayed, I felt my inward battle to believe being conquered by an overwhelming desire to make a difference. I dared to believe God would do something bigger than I could ever do on my own—birth a new beginning between men and women.

My heart began to break as I reflected on the countless women who had shared with me the painful places they had walked through with the men they loved. These good women of faith had wonderful hearts and believed in their marriages. Yet they had been left alone to battle for themselves and their children after their marriages were destroyed by infidelity, neglect, or abuse. Even the women who were determined to remain married battled to believe their marriages could ever be truly meaningful and reflect real love.

As I continued to pray about accepting this invitation, God brought back to my memory the painful night in my childhood when, as I shared with you earlier, my dad stumbled into my room with tears in his eyes and fear on his face as he knelt at the foot of my bed and broke the news that he and my mom were divorcing. I realize now that he had lost his will to fight and had no idea how to save his marriage or our family. Next I thought about my own marital struggles and the years of tears and trials it took for my husband, Steve, and me to rebuild a solid foundation for our marriage.

Then passion and compassion compelled me to take a step of faith in spite of my insecurities. I surrendered to this invitation in an effort to bring transformation to these men and their marriages. Once I committed to the date, I became desperate for God to give me the words, compassion, courage, and wisdom I would need to stand before these men.

To my surprise, God gave me much more than a message. He gave me a letter of repentance I was to deliver before my message. For the first time in my many years of ministry, I felt Him begin to break my heart for more than just women, but for our men as well. I realized they are just as frustrated as we are about our relationships with them.

I so wanted this event to be effective. After much prayer, I began to write the words the Lord led me to say. As I did, I could feel the tears begin to fall down my cheeks onto the paper. It suddenly hit me that the healing words God had given me were a direct reflection of many of the things I had said and done to my own husband and to the men I had dated during my single years. Up to this sobering moment, I had secretly blamed men for all the pain women were forced to walk through. I realized I had even blamed my own husband for all that was not right in our marriage.

The truth is I was so focused on my own feelings and so blinded by my marital battles that it had never occurred to me that my response to my husband's imperfections could be weakening his will and desire to lead in our marriage and might even be killing his confidence in Christ.

Don't get me wrong; we all know many men who have done some hurtful things to women. I have personally dedicated much of my life to writing books intended to heal women's hearts—including my own. However, we are losing our men of faith by the masses, and if nothing changes we will continue to lose our men of God. They need a breakthrough so they can become the men they long to be.

This is not an easy topic to write about, but it is an urgent matter. We need God to intervene and give our men a new beginning, knowing that they are more than the mistakes they have made. Then they can love and lead us the way God has appointed them to.

With that said, I invite you to read the opening letter on forgiveness I delivered with fear and trembling before these men, which I believe opened their hearts and ears to my message:

Dear Men of All Ages,

Now more than ever, we need you to rise up and fight for us, fight to remain faithful, and fight to finish strong! We need you to fight to leave a legacy of faith for the sake of our children and the foundation of marriage. Now I know this seems almost impossible in a society that screams "You have failed us in every way!" so I stand here today on behalf of all women and girls and ask that you forgive us for the following:

Forgive us . . .

for blaming you for all that has gone wrong in our lives and for making you pay the price for all the men who hurt us—even if it was not your fault.

Forgive us . . .

for holding on to the past and making you feel like you don't deserve to be forgiven or have a fresh start.

Forgive us . . .

for trying to conquer and compete with you . . . when we were created to complete you.

Forgive us . . .

for the way our words and our actions have publicly dishonored, discouraged, and disrespected you.

(continued)

Forgive us . . .
for using our beauty and our bodies to weaken your flesh and control you.

Forgive us . . .
for all the mind games we have played with you and the manipulation we have used to get your love and attention.

Forgive us . . .
for forgetting to make you feel like the heroic man we desire you to be in our lives!

The reaction of the men astonished me. As I shared these words, the room was completely silent; it was surreal and a little scary. I had one eye on the paper and one eye on the men. It was as if each sentence lowered their defenses, and by the time I said the last word, many of the men even had tears in their eyes. Their faces seemed to say, "Please unlock the hero inside me" and "Show me how to become the man I long to be to my wife and family."

I took a deep breath and then respectfully asked their permission to speak into their lives about their relationships with their wives. I asked if I could help them understand the heart of a woman; to attempt to explain how we are wired and what we need from them to feel safe, secure, and loved.

I assured them my goal was to give them Christ-centered, creative ways they could rescue, romance, replenish, and repair the women they had possibly hurt. I was taken aback by their response: the men stood to their feet and gave me a standing ovation before I even began sharing my message.

Something in the words that God had given to me unlocked the hero inside their hearts, and I could see they were willing to hear whatever I had to share. That opening letter accomplished God's mission as they left inspired to fight again for the women they love.

Even though I knew those words came to me through divine intervention, I have to be honest with you, I did not "feel" like speaking those words of life. I have heard so many women tell tragic love stories involving abuse and abandonment that I secretly feared this message might justify the hurts men have caused or give them an excuse for their actions. Today, I know it is not about what I see, hear, or feel; it is about doing whatever we can to rebuild broken lives.

Our God proved His faithfulness that day as the men left inspired to love their wives again. After the event, I received hundreds of e-mails from wives, ex-wives, and daughters thanking me for what was said and done in their men that weekend.

I once heard a pastor say, "If you are struggling to respect your husband, find the strength to respect him as your brother in the Lord." That comment really woke me up as I realized that none of us really deserves honor or respect except the Lord. Honor and respect are powerful tools to rebuild a broken society, but how do we show respect and honor to those who act disrespectful and do dishonorable things? What can we do to cultivate honor and respect between men and women again, and how can we influence our children to live in a way that is honorable to God and respectful of people?

Yes, our men may have done many things that certainly do not deserve to be honored, but they are God's children just like we are and they are imperfect just like we are. We women are not responsible for their dishonorable actions, but one way we can each help rebuild our broken men is to treat them like the men they want to become.

As I shared with you in an earlier chapter, my husband and I owned a Christian production company, which produced talent showcases for aspiring models, actors, and singers. But more important than exposing these potential stars to Hollywood was the ministry time that took place during the week of rehearsals and workshops, as we would share God's love and plan of salvation for their lives.

During one particular showcase in Seattle, a group of gang members hung around outside the room where we were holding the auditions. They made fun of each of the participants as he or she walked out of the audition. It was obvious they were there to cause trouble. I struggled with fear and anger as I prayed for protection over the young adults walking out to their cars. Then something happened as I made eye contact with one of the boys through the glass doors I was standing behind. My heart began to break with compassion, and my faith overpowered my frustration. My mother's heart thought, *Maybe these boys have never seen a woman or man honor and respect one another. Maybe they just need someone to treat them like they were made for more.*

God grabbed hold of my mother's heart, and I began to look at these boys through different eyes. I realized I didn't know their pasts, their parents, or their present circumstances, but I did know they were truly loved by God, no matter how disrespectfully they were behaving.

I took a step of faith and invited these boys to spend a week taking acting workshops at no charge. Their first response was, "Why would anyone do something for us?" However they couldn't resist the offer.

Each day when they would walk into the room for their workshop I would stand to my feet, walk over to greet them at the door, and treat them like guests of honor. The first day I took them around and introduced them to each of our staff members.

The next day I decided to make lunch for them. Although I did not like the way they acted or the words that were coming out of their mouths, I decided I would make every effort to use whatever influence I had as a woman to inspire them to live honorable lives. To my surprise the power of prayer, honor, and respect paid off as I witnessed these boys begin to transform. Not only did they begin to act differently, I learned a valuable lesson that week: honor is not something someone has to earn. It is an attitude I need to learn to give to all those God has created, including my own husband.

Don't get me wrong; I know it is not easy to keep an attitude of honor and respect in a dishonorable world, and it's even harder to treat someone who has hurt us with any respect. But honor creates an atmosphere that will bring glory to God and protect our hearts from becoming like the world around us.

We are not responsible for the dishonorable actions of our men. They will answer to God for their own actions, but we certainly do not have to become dishonorable and disrespectful women. We can use our God-given influence whenever we have a chance, if for no other reason than for the world to see what honor looks like. If we influence only one person, or if we validate only one person's existence by our respectful attitude, we will have made a difference in this world.

I know many of us are afraid to treat our men with an attitude of honor because we feel we will enable them to continue doing dishonoring things. First, I want to say the word *honor* doesn't mean doormat. We can be completely honest regarding how we feel about our men's actions and still remain respectful. If anything, respectful confrontation gives us a better chance at getting our men to hear our hearts. By our attitude and actions, we can help our men see who they can become. They won't always hear or change; however, by choosing to act honorably, we will not allow their actions to turn us into dishonorable women. Even if our men don't change, our hearts will remain untainted by their actions because of our obedience. And when we honor our husbands, we honor God.

LOVE COACHING

Respect yourself . . .

Love each other with genuine affection, and take delight in honoring each other.
ROMANS 12:10

Honoring is an action of obedience—not a feeling. Yet it does not mean we ignore the hurts we've suffered. Part of our society's decay comes from women not respecting themselves. Men crave respect from a woman, but they also want a woman who respects herself. Just think what would happen if we began to respect ourselves and respect others.

As the neck turns, so does the head. If we show honor, men will be drawn to respect us because we will not be settling for less than God has for us. From this day forward, let's not settle for second best. Let's not contribute to a dishonoring society, but instead do all we can to show honor and respect to every man as well as ourselves.

❧ Think about the Cross . . .

My old self has been crucified with Christ. It is no longer I who live, but Christ lives in me. So I live in this earthly body by trusting in the Son of God, who loved me and gave himself for me.
GALATIANS 2:20

When we struggle to respect someone who does not deserve it, let's take a moment to reflect on the Cross. You and I did nothing to deserve forgiveness nor did we earn the right to enter heaven, but our heavenly Father chose us. I am praying that this truth gives all of us a bigger perspective on how important we are to God whether we act like His children or not. We will need the Lord's help to instill honor back in our society and in our homes. Even if our men don't act in a way that deserves honor or respect, you and I can choose to glorify God with our actions and reactions.

❧ Cultivate an attitude of honor . . .

If you serve Christ with this attitude, you will please God, and others will approve of you, too.
ROMANS 14:18

I've discovered that honor and respect are attitudes even more than actions. Think about how we act when we meet people we consider important. We don't act casually as if they don't matter. We put effort into treating them with honor, whether through a soft answer, a word of encouragement, or eye contact that says, "You are of worth to God."

🌿 Decide to honor in your heart . . .

Whatever is in your heart determines what you say.
MATTHEW 12:34

Honor and respect are decisions of the heart; in other words, we must make a conscious effort to pour honor and respect into others, not because they deserve honor and respect but because our heavenly Father asks us to treat people that way. Why should we allow dishonorable actions to cause us to act like dishonoring, disrespectful women? If we conform to the disrespectful ways of this world, waiting for others to change their behavior before we become women who honor and respect them, it will never happen. And yet I have found that people become the way we treat them.

🌿 Add value . . .

Others were given in exchange for you. I traded their lives for yours because you are precious to me. You are honored, and I love you.
ISAIAH 43:4

Honor adds value to others. Unmerited honor, giving eye contact or a handshake, makes others know their existence matters. Most people today feel invisible, as if their lives don't matter. When we stand when they walk into the room or tune in to what they're talking about or respect the way that they think, it transforms them because it gives them the ability to see themselves the way God does. Honor and respect are about so much more than us; they're about redirecting people's lives and depositing a sense of honor in our society. God gives us unmerited honor. Let's do the same for His creation and for His glory.

LET US PRAY

Dear God,

Please forgive me for dishonoring others out of my anger and frustration with them. You know my heart and You know how hard it is for me to honor someone who has hurt me or hurt others, but I know how powerful an impact it makes when I do what You ask me to do. First, I ask that You would deal with my heart that I may become a woman of honor and a woman who respects others. Next, I lift the men in my life before You and ask You to help them become men of honor. I pray this prayer by faith in Jesus' name. Amen.

Therefore, as God's chosen people, holy and dearly loved, clothe yourselves with compassion, kindness, humility, gentleness and patience.
COLOSSIANS 3:12, NIV

His Love Letter to You

My Beloved Daughter,

I know you live in a world that does many dishonorable things, and that breaks My Father's heart. I am asking you to become a woman of honor by your actions and reactions toward others. You are not of this world, so I don't want you to allow the attitudes and actions of those in this world to mold you. I want to be the One who leads you to live a life of honor that is a reflection of My grace and love for mankind. Look to Me, not to man, and you will find what is truly worthy of honor.

Love,
Your King who honors you

Bear with each other and forgive one another if any of you has a grievance against someone. Forgive as the Lord forgave you. And over all these virtues put on love, which binds them all together in perfect unity.

COLOSSIANS 3:13-14, NIV

TREASURE OF TRUTH

HONOR IS A BEAUTIFUL ATTITUDE THAT ADDS
VALUE TO ALL THOSE WE LOVE AND CREATES
AN ENVIRONMENT THAT GLORIFIES OUR GOD.

Love Questions for Your Small Group

1. Describe your reaction to the letter of repentance Sheri Rose read to the men at the conference "What Women Want."

2. What are some creative ways that we can bring honor for our men back into our homes and society?

Love Question Online with Sheri Rose

Is it possible for me to confront my man without dishonoring him? If so, how?

Snap the code with your smartphone or visit the link for Sheri Rose's insights.

www.tyndal.es/YourHeartsDesire13

FOR MORE TEACHING VIDEOS FROM SHERI ROSE,
GO TO WWW.BIBLELIFECOACHING.COM.

14

DESIRING TO SURRENDER MY WHOLE HEART TO MY LORD

Fighting to Give Up My Wants for God's Will in My Life

And I saw the holy city, the new Jerusalem, coming down from
God out of heaven like a bride beautifully dressed for her husband.

REVELATION 21:2

IN THIS FINAL CHAPTER, I want to talk to you as a spiritual mom, as if you were my own daughter. I want you to know I pray you do find the love you're looking for in a godly relationship with your husband or, if you're single, with the man God may have for you. However, with that said, I don't want you to waste another day living as a woman in waiting who needs a man to begin her life.

I want you to be free to embrace life now. Life and love are not easy; that is why we need our Savior. If not now, at some point in this life, every one of us will be faced with a choice. Will we choose to continue to follow Christ by living life in a way that says "I do" and "I will finish strong at any cost"?

When my family faced its greatest attack a few years ago, I was forced to make a decision. Would I surrender my heart's desire to God's desire and say, "I do and I will follow Him at any cost"?

In a moment of truth, I decided I would not waste the spiritual war I was in, so I painfully committed to finish what God had for me, with or without the family I longed for.

That meant laying my family down at the feet of Jesus and making a commitment to follow Him for better or for worse. That meant working through the layers of hurt, misunderstanding, and dashed expectations between my husband and me. The truth is this: passing on a legacy of faith means so much more than getting the life we want now. We all want "happily ever after," and it's coming when Christ returns.

However, if you're single, don't waste your life waiting for a man, or if you're married, don't wait for your man to change before you begin living out your faith. I know it is hard to imagine what it will be like the day Jesus, our true Prince, comes to rescue us from this world, so I invite you to wrap your heart around this final story. Let your heart dream as you read about the love of your life and *your* "heavenly wedding day," when your Prince (our Lord) will come to rescue you from this world.

Imagine with me the most glorious wedding day of all. . . .

The bride-to-be stands motionless, staring in the mirror

for what seems like an eternity. Her hair and makeup are like works of art, and her dress is pure and white as snow. Never before has she imagined she would feel so treasured by her Lord as she twirls around her dressing room with joy, excitedly waiting for the ceremony to begin. She begins to reflect on her life and the people God had placed in her path while she was walking on earth.

If only she had known that this dream would become reality when her Prince came. Then she would have made sure everyone she met know about the open-ended invitation from her Savior to experience His eternal love. She begins to weep as she realizes that, while waiting for a "happily ever after," she had lost sight of the coming grand finale of her everlasting life. In her search for a man to love her, she had forgotten to embrace the one true Prince who gave Himself for her to experience this day.

It hits her suddenly like a stabbing jolt of reality: He had done everything to prepare for this day. He had done everything to woo her, to bless her, to capture her heart, to rescue her . . . and she had done nothing! She has nothing to offer Him. No gifts. No guests. She spent her life worrying about all the wrong things and living for all the wrong reasons. The depth of her regret is so intense that she grabs the hem of her gown and turns, ready to run away.

But just then she hears the sound of the most beautiful music she has ever heard. The wedding march has begun! Then large double doors open into the most incredibly decorated sanctuary she has ever seen. She sees angels singing glory to the Lord. She hesitantly walks down the aisle of the glorious sanctuary as she fights to believe this could really be happening. She feels so undeserving of such a celebration, yet she cannot help but absorb the indescribable beauty surrounding her. Then, suddenly, everything around her seems to blur as she catches sight of her Savior for the first time.

He looks so tender and loving, standing there at the end of the aisle, patiently waiting for His bride to approach. There are no bridesmaids or groomsmen, only her Groom and what appears to be an amazing number of wedding presents. She had heard that her Prince had prepared many gifts for His bride, but this is truly beyond what she could have imagined.

An intense flood of emotion overflows in her heart. As she approaches her Groom—her Prince—she feels her heart beating fast and her face becoming flush with embarrassment for not living a better life for Him. Just as she is ready to run, her eyes meet His.

She sees something in His loving eyes that is more intense than her shame, more powerful than her guilt. This "something" is stronger than anything she has ever felt before. His presence is irresistible, and no emotion can keep her from walking toward Him. As she keeps her eyes fixed on His, her shame begins to melt away, and the closer she gets to her Lord, the more sure she is that the look on His face is one of pure love, the kind of love that says, "You are Mine, My beloved bride, and nothing you have ever said or done could diminish My never-ending love for you."

As she steps up to stand next to her Groom, every

negative emotion loosens its grip on her and departs forever. Every pain that has burrowed its way into her soul disappears. As they stand there face-to-face, she realizes that she has always been loved, and for the first time she really experiences His love the way He wants her to. The Prince smiles at her and reaches out His hand and gently wipes away the tears from her cheek. He then wraps His loving arms around her and whispers, "You will never cry again, My love. Welcome home."

When we know Jesus as our Savior, then He is our Prince, we are His bride, and this story is about the majestic day of His return. Let's not wait; let's get ready for our Prince and live our lives in a way that tells the world we are loved. We have nothing to lose in this life if we say "I do" and "I will" follow the Prince who gave His life for me. If we believe the Word of God and embrace eternity, it becomes effortless to surrender our hearts to His love and His will. He is coming to rescue us; the question is, will we be ready?

LOVE COACHING

I'm not sure what you've walked through or who holds the key to your heart, but if you will hand that key to the Lord, you will find the safe place you're longing for. Your security will no longer be based on others' actions. Even those who love you the most don't know how to love you the way your Lord does. Just listen to His promise in Revelation 21:4: "He will wipe every tear from their eyes, and there will be no more death or sorrow or crying or pain. All these things are gone forever."

FINDING YOUR HEART'S DESIRE

If you're married . . .

I know it's hard to say "I do" and "I will" when you have stood in the gap for your marriage and believed God for restoration and it hasn't happened.

The truth is, you are a beautiful chosen bride of Christ, and in this life there will be trouble. But you have a real Prince. His name is Jesus, and He has felt every pain you've ever experienced. He endured rejection and crucifixion so you would have the power to finish your life and have everlasting life with Him.

Yes, we want to pray for our men and we want to empower them with our words, our actions, our influence, and our prayers. But we cannot allow any man on this earth to keep us from the ultimate relationship with our Lord. There is such security for our hearts when we fall for the One who gave His life for ours.

Please know I am not in any way encouraging you to divorce your husband to follow Christ, but you don't have to wait for your husband to change before you begin changing the world around you.

There is something so much more satisfying in fighting for the things that matter, than fighting with a man to get him to love you.

🌿 *If you're single . . .*

I know it's also hard to say "I do" and "I will" to Christ if you're single and have believed God for an amazing husband—only to be let down by the men you meet. But if you determine to follow Christ at any cost and if you will allow Him to love you, His presence will satisfy your soul. You will begin to dance through this life with Him, feeling His heart beat for your life here on earth. As wonderful as it seems to have a man to love you, you don't need a man to make a difference in this world. As a matter of fact, the apostle Paul says it's better not to marry so you can do the work of the Lord without distractions.

Don't put your purpose on "pause" while you wait for a man to push the "play" button. It's time to let the Lord push the "play" button so you will be free to live today with passion and joy, even as you are driven by eternity. If you will stop looking for a spouse to make you complete and let the Lord fill you up, I believe your open heart will be ready to receive the kind of man God has designed for you to have. I would even go so far as to say you will become much more attractive to a godly man if you are more concerned about your relationship with God than about any dating relationship.

No matter how much you love someone, he can never give you the intimacy you crave the way your Lord can. I know it's hard to embrace an invisible Prince, but the more you sing love songs to Him, the more you pray, the more you are in the Word, and the more you call out to Him, the more real He will become to you. I am praying and believing that your Prince Jesus will become enough for you to feel complete and cared for.

This is your beautiful life. Don't waste another minute waiting on a man before you live it! It's time to take a step of faith, lean on your Lord, and leave the desires of your heart in His hands so you can step into your divine destiny now and be a part of furthering His Kingdom on earth. Some will reject your invitation, but others will forever thank you for leading them to the entrance of heaven.

In Closing

I believe if the Lord was going to write you a personal love letter from heaven out of 1 Corinthians 2:9, it might read like this. . . .

His Love Letter to You

My Eternal Bride,

I long to be the One whom you crave so I can give you a true picture of My eternal love for you. There is not a man on earth who can quench your thirst for love like I can. Whatever you are looking for to feel secure, I am the One who can provide perfect peace even in the hardest of times. If you will fully open your heart to Me, you will feel Me walking you through every step of your life.

One day soon you will see Me face-to-face. On that glorious day, I will carry you over the threshold of this life and into the heavenly house I am preparing for you. Now look to the future with hope, My beloved bride, and allow Me, your true Prince, to reveal Myself to you in extraordinary ways.

Love,
Your Savior, the One who gave His life for you!

No eye has seen, no ear has heard, and no mind has imagined what God has prepared for those who love him.

1 CORINTHIANS 2:9

PRAYER FOR PERSONAL SALVATION

I want to take a moment to invite you to give your heart fully to the Lord and receive His gift of everlasting life if you have not already. Maybe you have known Him from afar but never experienced a personal, intimate relationship with Him. If you are ready to receive a new life in Christ and a real happily ever after in heaven, I invite you to say this prayer for salvation:

Dear Jesus,

My heart's desire is to be closer to You. Thank you for dying on a cross for me. Please forgive me for anything I have done to sin against You. I am taking a step of faith and inviting you now to come into my heart and be the Lord of my life. Even though I don't fully understand I want to learn what it means to live my life for You so I ask You now to write my name in Your Book of Life and crown me with the eternal crown of everlasting life as I acknowledge that you are Lord of Lords and King of Kings. In Your name I pray, amen.

WEDDING VOWS
TO MY LORD AND PRINCE

As we close our time together, wouldn't it be amazing to marry our heart to our Lord and our Prince, who gave His life for us and is coming back to rescue us from this world? After all . . . *we are His beloved bride.*

My Lord, Today I say "I do" and "I will" take You as my heavenly Husband from this day forward . . .

 I take You, Jesus, for better or for worse
 In times of sickness and in times of health
 In times of triumph and in times of trial
 In times of joy and in times of sorrow
To have and to hold until You return or death places me in Your arms, where I will see you face-to-face and my heart's desire will finally be fulfilled.
Amen!

Let us be glad and rejoice, and let us give honor to him.
For the time has come for the wedding feast of the Lamb,
and his bride has prepared herself.

REVELATION 19:7

TREASURE OF TRUTH

HIS LOVE FOR US IS AN EVERLASTING
LOVE THAT WILL NEVER COME TO AN END!

Love Questions for Your Small Group

1. As you read the wedding vows to Christ, which promise was the hardest for you to make?
2. How does it feel to know you're the bride of Christ and that you will spend eternity with Him in heaven?

Love Question Online with Sheri Rose

 How I can have an intimate relationship with an invisible God?

Snap the code with your smartphone or visit the link for Sheri Rose's insights.
www.tyndal.es/YourHeartsDesire14

FOR MORE TEACHING VIDEOS FROM SHERI ROSE,
GO TO WWW.BIBLELIFECOACHING.COM.

CHAPTER HIGHLIGHTS
TO HOLD ON TO

1. Desiring a "Happily Ever After"

FIGHTING THE TEMPTATION TO GIVE UP ON LOVE
AND MARRIAGE

Love never gives up, never loses faith, is always hopeful, and endures through every circumstance.
1 CORINTHIANS 13:7

I don't know where you stand today with the man you love or loved—or whether you are single, divorced, separated, or widowed. Still, I ask you to consider taking a step of faith with me and begin building a new foundation of love.

I have discovered that healing can begin and hope is restored if we use our pain to bring change and allow God to give us a picture bigger than our own wants and desires. We can use our mistakes to make us wiser and our pain to make us passionate to devote our lives to a purpose greater than our own personal happiness.

We can think about it this way. Even if we have lost all faith in all men or the man we once loved, we can keep faith in our Lord, who showed this love by offering His life for us on a cross and who longs to meet our deepest heart's desire . . . to be loved and give love!

2. Desiring a Godly Man to Marry (for Singles)

FIGHTING NOT TO SETTLE FOR LESS THAN GOD'S BEST FOR ME

The LORD directs the steps of the godly. He delights in every detail of their lives.
PSALM 37:23

If you are single, I don't want you to settle for second best, so keep this list in the forefront of your mind. You might even consider printing it out and putting it in your Bible.

The wise woman's love checklist:

1. Look at the way a man loves his mother, because it is the way he will eventually love his wife.
2. Pay attention to the way he reacts when there is stress or conflict.
3. Meet his friends, keeping in mind that the people he hangs with are a reflection of his heart.
4. Pay attention to what your good friends see in him, because often those who love you can see better than you can see when you're falling in love.
5. Look at what he reads and what he watches on television, because they will be a reflection of his moral fiber.

6. Do your best not to be too physical, because it will cloud your vision and confuse your heart.

7. It is imperative that he respects your boundaries without challenging them.

8. Ask him to pray for you often, because you will need a man who knows how to cover you in prayer.

9. Ask yourself whether you feel at home when you're with him or whether you act like someone you're not to get him to like you.

10. Before you say "I do," go through premarital counseling with a pastor.

3. Desiring to Leave a Legacy for My Loved Ones

FIGHTING TO GIVE AN EVERLASTING BLESSING TO MY BROKEN FAMILY

I have fought the good fight, I have finished the race, I have kept the faith. Now there is in store for me the crown.
2 TIMOTHY 4:7-8, NIV

The way we face and fight our battles in this life will become our legacy. Maybe we're not living the life we dreamed about, but the legacy isn't about getting what we want; it is about giving what we have.

What good is getting our way, if we are not doing God's will? The greatest testimony is not how we start but how we finish . . . in God's strength you and I can leave a legacy of faith!

4. Desiring God's Design That Me and My Man Become One

FIGHTING TO FIND A HEART CONNECTION
IN OUR DRAMATIC DIFFERENCES

As iron sharpens iron, so one person sharpens another.
PROVERBS 27:17, NIV

Many times we react to what we feel, not what is real, and if we are hurting we rarely react in a way that will bring resolution.

Let's pray for perspective so we will not lose sight of what we're fighting for. Conflict comes no matter whom we marry. We may be fighting about different things with different men, but there will always be major differences between men and women. The key is not to try to change one another but to discover how to become one. The beauty of our differences will be found when we learn to embrace them.

5. Desiring God to Give Me the Power to Remain Pure

FIGHTING TO FIND THE BENEFITS AND
BLESSINGS OF PURITY

Run from sexual sin! No other sin so clearly affects the body as this one does. For sexual immorality is a sin against your own body.
1 CORINTHIANS 6:18

It isn't fair for us to expect our men to remain pure when we are using their weakness—our bodies—to grab their attention so we can feel good about ourselves. Many of us are doing more than grabbing their attention; we're taking their focus off their families for our own benefit. I don't mean to be harsh, but how many more men have to fall before we wake up? How will our sons and daughters find the strength to remain pure and experience a pure love if no one leads the way? Something has to change, and it has to start with us.

With that said, you and I shouldn't beat ourselves up for the past. Our amazing God gives us amazing grace, mercy, and new beginnings. We are His princesses, and our purity can begin today. He loves us and will do great things through us if we will purify ourselves for His glory from this day forward!

6. Desiring to Give and Receive Love
FIGHTING FEELINGS OF WORTHLESSNESS

May you experience the love of Christ, though it is too great to understand fully. Then you will be made complete with all the fullness of life and power that comes from God.
EPHESIANS 3:19

How we feel will never change how our heavenly Father feels about you and me. Our hearts will always deceive us, but God's truth will clear the way so we can see our value through heaven's eyes.

I don't know where you've been or what hinders you from believing you are worthy of love, but I do know the Lord gave His life to prove your worth. And you are indeed worthy to receive His great love for you.

7. Desiring to Embrace My New Life in Christ
FIGHTING THE ENEMIES OF SHAME, GUILT, AND REGRET

At that moment their eyes were opened, and they suddenly felt shame at their nakedness. So they sewed fig leaves together to cover themselves.
GENESIS 3:7

As hard as it is to believe, God truly can take even shameful things we have done and somehow use them for His glory. We don't have to continue to live in shame any longer. Yes, we live in a fallen world, and yes, we sometimes fall into the temptations of this world. The truth is we are more than the mistakes we make, and it isn't just about what we have done. It is about what has been done for us on the cross!

8. Desiring to Become a Woman My Man Can Lead
FIGHTING TO LET GO AND TRUST HIS LEADERSHIP

But there is one thing I want you to know: The head of every man is Christ, the head of woman is man, and the head of Christ is God.
1 CORINTHIANS 11:3

God created men to be the captains of the ship, and we women are the radar. He is the head . . . we are the neck that turns the head.

We have two challenges going on at the same time.

Our men want to lead but don't feel they can lead well, and we want our men to lead but don't feel we can trust their leadership.

Even if we can lead better, what are we accomplishing if we are crippling them from being the leaders they are called to be? No matter how it appears, every man wants to be a strong leader, but many men are never given the chance to step into their God-appointed position.

9. Desiring My Son to Grow to Become a Man of Faith

FIGHTING MY FEARS OF FAILING AS HIS MOTHER

And she made this vow: "O LORD of Heaven's Armies, if you will look upon my sorrow and answer my prayer and give me a son, then I will give him back to you. He will be yours for his entire lifetime."
I SAMUEL 1:11

I know it's hard to believe our sons will ever be victorious over the temptations of this world. After all, so many men have been defeated by the giants of pornography, money, lust, and selfish living. We will need to pray and prepare our boys for battle so they see the giants from David's perspective.

David didn't see the giant as too big to hit . . . he saw him as too big to miss!

10. Desiring a Miracle to Build a New Foundation of Love

FIGHTING TO FIND A RENEWED PASSION, PURPOSE, AND PLAN

You know very well what trouble we are in. Jerusalem lies in ruins, and its gates have been destroyed by fire. Let us rebuild the wall of Jerusalem.
NEHEMIAH 2:17

I know it is hard to believe one person's love and reaction to the ruins of relationships will help rebuild our broken society; however, the rebuilt wall of Jerusalem was accomplished one stone at a time. Our God can and will rebuild a beautiful life out of any willing broken heart. He will use one sacrificial choice, one act of forgiveness, one sincere repentant heart, one woman who is willing to step out in faith and start rebuilding from the wreckage.

The truth is, we all hold a stone from the wreckage of relationships. Even if it is not our own relationship with a man, we are affected by the wreckage of our society's divorce rate and so are our children. It's time to stop talking about the ruins of relationships and start praying for the passion and wisdom to start rebuilding.

11. Desiring Expressions of Love and Romance in My Marriage

FIGHTING TO REMAIN FAITHFUL IN MY HEART

How lovely are your cheeks;
your earrings set them afire!
How lovely is your neck,
enhanced by a string of jewels.
We will make for you earrings of gold
and beads of silver.
SONG OF SONGS 1:10-11

I wonder how many affairs would not happen if husbands and wives were filling each other up instead of taking each other for granted. How much more would we be able to influence the world around us to believe in marriage again if we would publicly display our love for one another? What an amazing witness that would be!

12. Desiring to Believe God Can Change a Man and Save a Marriage

FIGHTING TO FORGIVE AND FORGET THE FORMER THINGS

Forget the former things;
*   do not dwell on the past.*
See, I am doing a new thing!
ISAIAH 43:18-19, NIV

A broken man can become a better man if he is given a chance. If a man is sincerely wounded, repentant, and wants to rebuild his life with his wife, it may be worth giving him another chance. It takes great courage for a man to come out of hiding and face his family, confess his sin, and cling to his wife again.

It would be a tragedy to let other women reap the benefits of the pain we had to go through when our men hurt us.

13. Desiring to Glorify God by Showing Honor and Respect

FIGHTING THE FRUSTRATION CAUSED BY DISHONORABLE ACTIONS AND ATTITUDES

Respect everyone, and love your Christian brothers and sisters. Fear God, and respect the king.
1 PETER 2:17

When we honor others, we are honoring our God.

Even if our men don't change, our hearts will remain untainted by their actions because of our obedience. There is something more powerful in doing the right thing than acting out disrespectfully.

When we honor and respect someone with our attitude and our actions, we help him to see who he can become and we protect ourselves from becoming like him.

14. Desiring to Surrender My Whole Heart to My Lord

FIGHTING TO GIVE UP MY WANTS FOR GOD'S WILL IN MY LIFE

And I saw the holy city, the new Jerusalem, coming down from God out of heaven like a bride beautifully dressed for her husband.
REVELATION 21:2

I know it's hard to say "I do" and "I will" when you have stood in the gap for your marriage and believed God for restoration and it never happened, or if you're single and you've believed God for an amazing husband and all you've met are men who have let you down.

The truth is, you are a beautiful chosen bride of Christ. And in this life there will be trouble, but you have a real Prince. His name is Jesus, and He has felt every pain you've ever experienced. He endured rejection and crucifixion so you would have the power to finish your life and have everlasting life with Him.

YOUR HEART'S DESIRE

As we close our time together, I would like to invite you to document for yourself and your Lord your heart's desire for the following things . . .

- Your heart's desire for your legacy

- Your heart's desire for your loved ones

- Your heart's desire for how you want your life to be remembered by those who watched you live out your faith

Write out a love letter or a prayer to your Lord.

> *Delight yourself in the LORD;*
> *and He will give you the desires of your heart.*
> PSALM 37:4, NASB

CLOSING WORDS FROM
Sheri Rose . . .

IT IS AMAZING TO ME how our God can take what appears to be the end and use it to build a strong foundation of faith for our children and ourselves. Think about what you've walked through when it comes to love. Now picture yourself using that pain as a tutor to make you wiser and to share that wisdom with someone you love.

Our Father in heaven has all we need to turn our pain into divine purpose and our despair into divine destiny for us and our beloved men. Don't forget that Jesus' family tree includes the prostitute Rahab. Don't forget that Solomon, whose father, King David, seduced his married mother, Bathsheba, and had her first husband, Uriah, killed, became the wisest man who ever lived. If God could redeem broken people like Rahab, David, and Bathsheba, He can certainly take whatever we have done or whatever has been done to us and redeem it too. With God, life's battles and brokenness do not have to be the end. They may be the very things that birth a new beginning.

When Jesus gave His life on the cross, it looked ugly. He was beaten, He was bruised, and He was broken for us. If it hadn't been for His brokenness we would not have a heavenly home to live happily ever after in when we get to heaven. We would not have the power of the Holy Spirit inside of us to persevere through painful places in our lives. We would not know the peace that passes all understanding.

Thank you for the privilege of pouring this message out on the pages for you to receive. My prayer is that you will never be the same.

Dear Lord,

I lift up my sister princess before You. I pray that You give her the desire of her heart. I pray she would embrace Your everlasting love for her. Help her keep her eyes fixed on eternity and fill her up with Your glory. May all she has ever done or experienced become a trophy of Your grace in her life. Amen.

I believe God will answer the prayer above, and if I never meet you on earth, I so look forward to celebrating your life and legacy in heaven. Until then, never forget who you are in Christ and how much you are truly loved by the King of kings.

Love,
Sheri Rose
WWW.BIBLELIFECOACHING.COM

ENDNOTES

96 "The man is the head" Nia Vardalos, *My Big Fat Greek Wedding* directed by Joel Zwick, Gold Circle Films, 2002.

124 "I had caused this" Bill McCartney and David Halbrook, *Sold Out: Becoming Man Enough to Make a Difference* (Nashville: Word, 1997), 209.

124–125 "Before that he was the same" Laurie Goodstein, "A Marriage Gone Bad Struggles for Redemption," *New York Times*, October 29, 1997.

125 "Do you *really* want to know" Bill McCartney, *Sold Out*, 230.

SCRIPTURE INDEX

MORE FROM THE AUTHOR

Online Bible Life Coaching with Sheri Rose

If you would like more insight on relationships or if you want to start a small group using the videos that go with this book, visit Sheri Rose at biblelifecoaching.com or e-mail her at rose@hisprincess.com.

More of
Your Heart's Desire

YOUR **H**EART'S **D**ESIRE **G**ROUP **E**XPERIENCE

- 7 love-coaching and Bible life-coaching sessions on DVD to go with the book

- A unique group experience for women's ministry studies or home groups with your daughters or a group of girlfriends, to help you grow in love

978-1-4143-7518-2; pack includes DVD and the book *Your Heart's Desire*

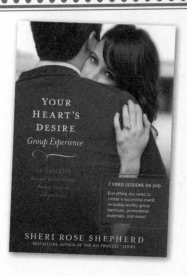

YOUR **H**EART'S **D**ESIRE **O**NLINE **L**OVE **C**OACHING

- 14 online coaching sessions with Sheri Rose to help you live out the truths in this book

YOUR **H**EART'S **D**ESIRE **W**OMEN'S **C**ONFERENCE

- Host a Your Heart's Desire Women's Conference at your church with Sheri Rose

- Hope, humor, and healing that will inspire every woman who has ever loved a man—married, widowed, single, or divorced

Real Life * *Real Love* * *Real Change*

CP0560

Bible Life Coaching

If you need some inspiration and want a mentor to keep you motivated, I would love to be your online coach, meet you at one of my conferences, or share more of my books with you. Please visit me at biblelifecoaching.com.

CP0562

In *My Beautiful Princess Bible,* Sheri Rose Shepherd helps girls learn what it means to be a daughter of the King of all kings!

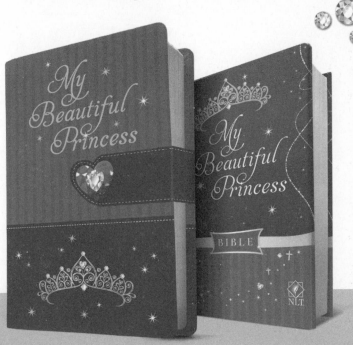

With feature-packed pages, Sheri Rose Shepherd shares a biblical perspective of being God's princesses, and helps girls discover the rich relationship they can have with God through the sacrifice of Jesus on the cross. All of the enhancements in this Bible were specially created to **engage girls in the Word of God** and **instill truth in their hearts** about who God is, how He sees them as His children, and that He has special plans for them!

Available editions:
Padded Hardcover ISBN 978-1-4143-6815-3
Purple Crown LeatherLike (with magnetic closure) ISBN 978-1-4143-7571-9
Deluxe Princess Pink/Purple Royalty LeatherLike (with magnetic closure)
ISBN 978-1-4143-6816-0

CP0561